"Although understanding how to comfort someone often only comes with living through difficult times, Nance's book helps you get started . . . taking those first steps toward helping someone in distress."
Niki Tsongas,
wife of the late U.S. Senator, Paul Tsongas

"After years of working with people in pain, I have heard too many 'unhealing' conversations. It's time for us to learn that one word of kindness to someone in pain can begin their recovery. This book teaches us how to pause long enough to listen into the silence of another's pain and to facilitate the body's potential to heal itself."
James Waslaski, past chair,
American Massage Therapy National Sports Massage Education Council

"In coaching managers to have difficult conversations, and having many of them myself, I realize that our fear in having that tough talk is actually worse than the conversation itself. [These] stories remove some of the stumbling blocks and once read, are transformed into personal courage."
Gwendy Longyear-Hayden, director,
Human Capital Solutions, Resources Connection

"Your book will help clergy like myself to be more attuned to what people in trouble are saying. It is a great teaching tool for me and for my colleagues."
Reverend Aram Marashlian, Secretary,
Massachusetts' Firefighters Chaplains Association

"Practical, friendly, and thoughtful guide for communication at home, school, and the workplace when confronting the challenge of healing broken relationships."
Badi G. Foster, president,
Phelps-Stokes Fund, former director of Tufts University's
Lincoln Filene Center for Citizenship and Public Affairs

Healing Conversations

Healing Conversations

What to Say
When You Don't Know What to Say

Nance Guilmartin

JOSSEY-BASS
A Wiley Company
www.josseybass.com

Published by

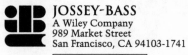

JOSSEY-BASS
A Wiley Company
989 Market Street
San Francisco, CA 94103-1741

www.josseybass.com

Jossey-Bass books and products are available through most bookstores. To contact Jossey-Bass directly, call (888) 378-2537, fax to (800) 605-2665, or visit our website at www.josseybass.com.

Substantial discounts on bulk quantities of Jossey-Bass books are available to corporations, professional associations, and other organizations. For details and discount information, contact the special sales department at Jossey-Bass.

We at Jossey-Bass strive to use the most environmentally sensitive paper stocks available to us. Our publications are printed on acid-free recycled stock whenever possible, and our paper always meets or exceeds minimum GPO and EPA requirements.

Library of Congress Cataloging-in-Publication Data

Guilmartin, Nance, date.
   Healing conversations : what to say when you don't know what to say / Nance Guilmartin.
      p. cm.
Includes bibliographical references and index.
   ISBN 0-7879-6019-5 (alk. paper)
   1. Consolation. 2. Interpersonal communication. I. Title.
   BF637.C54 G85 2002
   153.6—dc21   2001006624

FIRST EDITION
HB Printing 10 9 8 7 6 5 4 3 2 1

CONTENTS

THIS BOOK IS DEDICATED TO EACH OF YOU WHO,
IN A MOMENT OF UNCERTAINTY, TAKE THE CHANCE
TO OFFER OR TO ASK FOR A HEALING CONVERSATION.

AND, THIS BOOK IS DEDICATED TO CONNIE,
WHOSE WISDOM HELPED ME GO BEYOND . . .
WHEN I DIDN'T THINK I COULD.

An Invitation to Healing Conversations

HAVE YOU EVER WANTED TO HELP SOMEONE WHO'S GOING THROUGH A rough time but not known what to do or say? That's what happened to me one day when my best friend at work had her third miscarriage. Doctors had warned Shelley that another pregnancy could put her life at risk. Not having had children, I was at a loss for what to say and how to even *be* with my dear friend who kept risking her life trying to have a child.

Feeling inadequate but determined to find some way to be helpful, I got up the nerve to call the wife of a college friend who had lost her baby in a miscarriage. Even though I didn't know Rose all that well, I asked her if she would coach me in what might be helpful to say to someone who had lost a baby. "Don't talk a lot," Rose said. "Just listen. Don't try to come up with some simple answer to fix things. Don't think that telling a woman looking forward to motherhood that it was God's will or that she can adopt is comforting when she is coping with the sudden loss of her baby. As hard as it may be for you, don't try to make sense of it. Just let her talk . . . about anything."

One reason I wrote this book is that sooner or later, each of us will face a situation where we want to comfort people we care for but we don't know what to say or what to do or how to *be* with them. Or *we* may be the ones having a tough time and not knowing how to ask for or how to accept the help we need. This book is *not* a "self-help" guide. It's a guide for giving help to others *and* receiving comfort from them during life's inevitable awkward, messy, or poignant moments of uncertainty, transition, change, and loss. In the aftermath of September 11, 2001, the stories in this book become more pertinent to out daily lives—the realities of sudden death, near misses, losing a job through no fault of our own, or facing death in the workplace family. This book isn't about September 11, which happened as the book was going to press, but it may be that the event has heightened our awareness of the need for comfort and for healing conversations.

How *do* we learn to be with others' discomfort in a way that comforts them, no matter how awkward the situation is for them or for us? You learn at work one day that a colleague's parent has suddenly died or that several employees have been laid off or that one of your clients has cancer. Can you help? *Should* you help? What would be really useful? What kinds of boundaries do we respect or lower? How do we listen between the lines of silence to comfort someone who's afraid or in pain? Can we ask for what would comfort *us,* and are we able to receive it with grace?

It's hard for many of us to witness someone's pain or discomfort. We often want to fix it, take charge, provide instant relief somehow. Some of us, to avoid the risk of saying the wrong thing, say nothing. This book offers guidelines to help you bridge the communication gaps and make it easier to show that you care. These guidelines for action (or inaction) can also help you respond to the many situations not covered in these stories or respond when you feel unprepared or caught off guard. For example, a father who learns that his son is skipping school and getting into serious trouble should be able to use the principles expressed here to have a healing conversation even though there is no "school-skipping" story in the book.

The stories in this book are true experiences* shared in the hope that once you've read them, when you're called on to lend a hand or to lend an ear, you'll be able to provide what's really needed. Feel free to read the stories in any order you like—you may feel the need to turn to a particular story right away, or perhaps you will want to read the book from cover to cover to be prepared to respond with emotional first aid at a moment's notice.

This book isn't a guide to being correct. It's an invitation to *step into someone else's shoes* through personal stories that might help you offer, ask for, or receive comfort. Sometimes a story won't offer you much advice or guidance, for I believe that just by reading about another person's experience, you will be more sensitive to how someone might feel in that situation, and that in itself will help you know what to say or be with someone in a similar circumstance.

As storytellers, we're not counselors or psychologists giving you an expert opinion. We're offering our own experiences of what worked, what didn't, and what we wished we'd known to ask for at the time. The stories also invite you to pause to reflect on *your* needs before you try to help someone else.

Taking the time to pause is something I've had to learn how to do as a "breakthrough coach," helping companies and individuals shed new light on

*Some of the names and circumstances have been changed to protect privacy.

their problems. I've learned that at the heart of most business or relationship breakdowns is a miscommunication or a missed understanding. At those times of uncertainty, the most important "power tool" we can use is one most of us never had a course in: listening. "Reflections" at the ends of the chapters offer you a chance to pause—to imagine what you might do differently the next time you or someone you know needs comfort during a difficult time.

Make no mistake, there will be days when you aren't up to the task of listening without judging or offering comfort. There will also be times when you're not able to receive support despite someone's best intentions. These are the times when we learn that a healing conversation isn't just about hearts and flowers—it takes more than that to get yourself or others through difficult times. It takes work. It's risky. And above all, it takes a commitment to listen—to the silence, to the pain, and to the hope beneath the words. *To listen to where the heart lives.* To imagine that during those moments of trying to care or asking for help, we are holding another's heart in our hands.

The storytellers and I offer you what we've learned along the way, the mistakes we've made, and the lessons we've been taught. We hope you will share *your* stories and insights with others too.

Getting Started

*Supporting others without fixing,
rescuing, or judging*

CONVERSATIONS. WE HAVE THEM EVERY DAY. WE MAY REHEARSE WHAT WE'D like to say. Or we may just blurt out our thoughts. Before we know it, the rhythm begins, like a ping-pong game: I speak, you listen. You speak, I listen. My turn. Your turn. Ping-pong. Ping-pong. All the while, I'm thinking about what I'm going to say. You may be wondering what you're going to say. Eventually one of us starts wondering where this is leading. And yet we're trying to have a conversation. We speak. We listen. But do we ever really hear what someone meant or perhaps what they left unsaid? Are we able to say what's in our hearts? Can we listen through the layers of what someone is feeling? To what we are feeling, too?

When someone needs our help, or when we need theirs, it's easier than ever to just start talking or to say nothing at all. *How do we have a healing conversation of the heart, not just the head?* How can we show up for that conversation—body, mind, and soul?

When you want to comfort someone or you need comfort, the guidelines for healing conversations presented in this book may help when you are unsure of what to say or how to be. As you read the stories in these pages, you'll discover how you might listen; pause; be a friend, not a hero; offer comfort; be in touch with your feelings; be there over the long haul; show up even when it's awkward; be a helpful resource; take the initiative; and be compassionate.

A HEALING CONVERSATION GUIDE

Listen

Listening isn't just about being quiet. It's about listening to what people say, what they don't say, and what they mean. It's not about talking or asking questions either. Oddly enough, that's what a lot of us do when we think we're listening. We tell our stories or we ask things we want to know. Listening is about hearing with our eyes, our ears, and our heart without needing to know something right away. To do that we have to be willing to suspend the internal conversations. Those are the conversations going on inside our head where it's easy to get caught up in thinking about what we're going to say, reacting to what they're saying, or wondering where the conversation is going.

Pause

There's a time to speak and a time to listen between the lines. When we hear ourselves saying, "I don't understand . . . ," that's a clue to pause and ask,

"What am I missing here?" It takes a special commitment, though, to slow down our often automatic reaction to someone's need for comfort. Our mind wants to speed past the discomfort of their discomfort so without thinking about it, we'll often shift right into taking action—saying or doing something that we think can help.

Taking the time to pause and reflect allows us to stop judging, stop reacting, and get curious. It allows us to tap in to compassion at the very moment when, if we didn't pause, we might find ourselves saying something we'd later regret. There's a sense of timing in offering comfort. When the timing is right, the doors can open; when the timing is off, it may be a long time before they will open again. Pausing gives us the clues to determine whether or not this is a good time to offer support. Pausing is just like putting the clutch in when you are driving a car with a stick shift: it lets you slow down just enough to engage the gears before you speed up. The art of speaking is not just knowing the right thing to say at the right time but also not saying the wrong thing at the tempting time. When we can pause even briefly, to tune in to another person's often unspoken needs, it helps us tune out the internal conversations that may drive us to move too quickly into action.

Be a Friend, Not a Hero

Helping others get through a rough time isn't the same thing as rescuing them from a situation that is painful for them or for you. People have the right and the responsibility to come to terms with the consequences of their behavior, the behavior of others, and the difficult situations that may result. Healing conversations acknowledge their pain; let them feel it, and *don't try to rush it away.* We try to provide a bridge for them to cross their river of fear.

Offer Comfort

Giving comfort does not mean telling people how they should or shouldn't feel. No one can know how anyone else should feel. No matter what other people are feeling, they have a right to feel that way. Comfort means that we aren't judging them, aren't thinking of them as broken and in need of fixing. We are giving them room to be who they are and how they are at the time. We show them that we care *without needing to agree or disagree* with their choices or with how they are handling a difficult situation.

Be in Touch with Your Own Feelings

When we're busy trying to help others, we can forget that people pick up on our vibrations—on the unspoken thoughts and feelings going on inside of us. Though they can't know for sure what we're thinking, people can often sense whether we're panicking, judging them, or feeling sorry for them. Helping others feel comforted in our presence has a lot to do with what's going on inside of us. No matter what situation we face, a healing conversation gives others the gift of our presence. To offer that kind of support means that we are able to sit with our own discomfort long enough to be with theirs. We are able to offer compassion to them because we can also give it to ourselves.

Be There over the Long Haul

Change is messy. It can't be cleaned up in a hurry. People need time to adjust, to second-guess themselves, to transition, to ask "What if?" In a healing conversation, we learn to accept that sometimes a friend, a family member, a colleague, or a neighbor needs us to be nothing more than a sounding board—over and over again.

Show Up Even When It's Awkward

It's OK to be uncomfortable with feeling awkward in just about any situation. It's OK for us to let the person we're trying to support know how we feel, too. It's even fine for us to be honest enough to say, "Truly, I don't know how you feel or what to say, *and* I do care about you." If you are the one who needs to be comforted, even though you may feel funny about saying this, it's fine to let someone know that you're not up to talking right now. In either case, you may choose to let someone know how you feel by putting your thoughts in writing. A healing conversation doesn't always have to be conducted out loud.

Be a Helpful Resource

We don't have to have all the answers to other people's questions. Often the best thing we can do is refer them to another resource—another friend, an expert, a friend of a friend. We are sensible enough to know when we have reached the limits of our ability to provide support and are willing to suggest that people seek professional help. We can even call ahead to make that connection easier for them to pursue. We can also give them resources, such as books, or even lend them a place to escape to so that they can peacefully find their own answers.

Take the Initiative

When we ask people, "What can I do for you?" sometimes they'll have an answer, but sometimes they won't have a clue about how we can help. It's the things that they may *not* ask us for that can sometimes mean the most. Taking the time to put ourselves in their shoes to wonder what they'd be willing to accept from us, or taking responsibility for asking for what we need, can be the first step toward giving or receiving the care that's most helpful.

Be Compassionate

Even if we have been through a similar situation, we can't really know how someone feels. We can relate, maybe, but honestly, no one knows how someone else feels. We don't want to confuse empathy and sympathy with compassion. Remember to listen to others' stories before asking whether it would help to share yours.

Please be patient with yourself and others as you use these guidelines. The essence of healing is understanding and being understood. When the people you are trying to comfort feel understood and you have paused in ways that enable you to understand them a little better, you can experience a heart-to-heart moment. If that heartfelt connection is what you seek to give or receive, I invite you to use these ten principles to open the doors to intentional kindness.

Healing Conversations

CHAPTER ONE

When You Need a Friend

Please, Don't Ask Me How I Am, Unless . . .

❧ *Beginning a healing conversation*

How are you?

We ask that question all the time. It's usually a polite little greeting, just another way of saying hello. But we may not realize that this innocent-sounding greeting can cause stress for people who are going through difficult times. In these instances, it's important for us to be aware that when we ask that question, we need to consider if we're really willing to hear whatever the answer might be.

I had an unforgettable conversation with a woman whose mother was very ill. Maria's father had died a few months earlier, and her mother was at the point in her illness where she had signed a living will and was refusing life support. Maria's brother didn't agree with this decision. Maria was spending her days holding her brother's hand and comforting her mother. In the midst of all this, people were asking her, "How are you?"

"What goes through your mind is this," Maria explained. "You really want to know how I am? I'll tell you how I am. I feel like I'm losing it most of the time! I want to scream at my brother, scream at the doctors. I feel sad and empty. I've got to deal with medical policies, insurance, hospital administrators, my family, my mom, and somewhere in there my so-called normal life. So tell me, just how do I answer this question? Do I tell you how I really am? Or do I do what most of us do and smile or grimace a little and sigh, 'Oh, I'm fine, holding up.' Do I just keep the conversation flowing past any sticky points of emotional meltdown?"

Maria continued explaining how difficult it was for her to know what to say when people wanted to know how she was doing. "I know they mean well, but do you know what often happens? If I start to tell them how I really am, they interrupt and try to make me feel better by telling me their stories. Sometimes they want my sympathy for them. Sometimes they give me advice. Sometimes they try to take over and fix things. Sometimes they say, 'Oh,' and change the subject.

"What's hard is that I figure it's OK to say 'I'm fine' to the folks I don't really know, because I don't feel it would be fair to burden them with the truth. But with close friends, I'd like to be straight. Instead, sometimes I feel that it's my job to keep them from feeling too bad about what's happening with me. Most days, I say as little as possible and figure that no one really wants to know how I am. It would be too depressing, and they'd feel that they'd either have to walk away or try to fix things for me. All I really want is for people to listen to me. Not to fix. Not to advise. Not to tell me their stories yet. To be a harbor where I can bring my boat in and toss about and eventually settle down for a while."

Sometimes people want to talk and unload all the overwhelming, scary, frustrating stuff that's happening. Sometimes people would rather share a little silence with you. Other times it's nice for them to be able to say, "Right now I don't really want to talk about it—maybe later—but thanks for asking."

Struggling with "How are you?" can present an overwhelming number of choices of what to say and what not to say. It sounds like such a little thing, to avoid asking someone such an open-ended, all-encompassing question like "How are you?" To signal that you are open to hearing back from them something more than a weary "Fine," you can try "Do you want to talk about anything that happened today?" Or "Is there anything I can do to support you after the day you've had today?" Or "I don't know what to say right now, but I'd like you to know I care about you. Is there anything you want to talk about?"

People in difficult situations appreciate it when you don't ask them to give you the big picture. That's why asking them a question about how things are at this moment is easier than asking them how they are. Focusing in on the smaller picture enables them to tell you, "Well, at this moment, I'm OK; yesterday was rough, though." Or they could respond by saying something as straightforward as "Right now I could use a nap and a neck rub."

Another way to make an opening connection is to just let them know you care and that you aren't seeking information at all. You can tell them: "You've been in my thoughts." Or "I wish I were there to give you a hug, help you pack, take you where you need to go." Or "I've been trying to think of a way to support you. Would this help . . . ?"

Once the conversation is open, you might wonder what to say next. Remember that conversation isn't always a back-and-forth exchange, taking turns to talk and listen. It's not just about you being quiet so that then you can say what you've been thinking about while the other person was talking. *Heal-*

ing conversations are about pausing to tune in to what others need or want to say and what, if anything, they are able to hear from you at that moment. Healing conversations also make room for comfortably sharing silence.

There's another factor to consider when you want to take a healing conversation to the next level. Consider your relationship to the person. Sometimes the fact that you know each other well may make the person feel more comfortable in being blunt with you. Oddly enough, sometimes it will make the person feel *too* vulnerable. Don't assume you know which way someone else will feel. When you don't know someone well, you may actually be able to provide what is needed most: compassionate listening without judgment. If you are uncertain of how deep to get into a conversation with someone you don't know well, just pause and acknowledge, "I don't know you very well, but I'd like to do whatever I can to support you, even though I'm not sure what that would be. I'm willing to try." If you know the person well, you might take the conversation to the next level by reflecting what you sense your friend is feeling, not just what was said.

When people are having a rough time, usually the first question we ask them is "How are you?" because we think it's a way to open up the conversation and to show that we care. Here's another way to look at it: if you are trying to comfort people who are dealing with difficult situations, they will bless you for not making the "How are you?" question the first one. Ask about their work or their family or about almost anything else to give them a little relief from once again explaining what a rough time they are having getting through this trying experience. They want to be treated like whole individuals, not just as people in a challenging situation that is taking over their identity. Perhaps after listening carefully for a while, you may not even have to ask how they are because they will have told you in their own way.

Using the Rule of Six

🐚 *Asking for help*

Come on, now, how difficult can it be to ask for help? For some of us, it's difficult. For others, it's nearly impossible.

Most of us feel good when we can help others by doing things for them or saying things to comfort them or finding someone who can support them even better than we can. But when it comes to asking for help for ourselves, some of us find that doing so is almost more traumatic than the problems we're experiencing.

Years ago, two friends were working on a project together. They were walking around the block during a break. They were talking about dealing with the upsets in their lives—moving, career changes, divorce, health problems, and living on their own. One of them, like many of us, was so reluctant to ask for help that when help finally came, it was often too little too late. By then she'd be so desperate that she'd trust just about anyone and usually would wind up asking the wrong people to help her. Then there would be an extra price to pay for broken promises or unfulfilled expectations. So once again she would convince herself that it was less painful to go it on her own. She had been explaining her reluctance to ask for help when her friend, Dayashakti, a well-known spiritual teacher, asked her whom she was turning to for help.

Before she could complete her answer, Dayashakti stopped her and said, "You need to know about the Rule of Six," and proceeded to teach her an invaluable concept. The Rule of Six works like this. You have to ask six people for help. Not just one. Six! The first person you ask may be busy. The second may not want to get involved. The third may not be able to take care of your whole request. (By now, many of us would quit asking and decide, "I'll just do it myself.") The fourth person may refer you to someone else. The fifth can't do what you ask but can help in other ways. The sixth may be the one who, when you are good and ready to give up, simply says, "Sure, no problem, anything else I can do?"

Here are some commonsense guidelines for applying the Rule of Six:

- Not everyone you ask can actually help you.
- Not everyone you ask can help you in a way that you would find satisfactory.
- People you ask may offer to do only part of what you ask or may instead offer something you haven't asked for.
- People you ask may recommend someone else to assist you who would be better suited to the task.
- Asking several people for help may give you a range of options you wouldn't have had if you'd asked only one person to help you.

You are probably thinking, "That's it?" Just try it. See how easy, or hard, it is for you to graciously ask six people to help you. Try not to bail out when the first person isn't available or turns you down. It's so much easier not to ask than to be turned down or to deal with the awkwardness of people not doing what you'd asked but doing something else that they think will help.

Another reason many of us don't ask others for help is that we are thinking, "What can I ever do for them?" We don't want to be in other people's debt. What if we can't help them when they need us? Or we worry that asking for help may haunt us one day because now they'll be "expecting" something from us. We'd rather not take the risk of asking because we feel vulnerable about receiving help from others, about crossing a threshold of intimacy beyond which they might get to see a different side of us.

Here's what we forget: we forget how good we feel when we get to take others to the hospital when they need a ride, look after their dogs, pick up their kids, mow their (hilly!) lawns while they recover from surgery, or help track down financial, medical, or legal advisers to help them cope. We enjoy feeling that we have made a difference, yet we hesitate to allow others to do the same for us.

Friends who patiently taught me how to ask for and receive help have hammered one key point into my head: asking for help is merely a sign of being human. They are right. On the days when friends and clients know you are going through rough times, they may feel closer to you because, for a change, you don't seem to have it all together. You actually show that you need others. It turns out that when we don't ask for help, we think we are sparing people the trouble of doing something for us. In fact, if we would just ask them or accept their unsolicited offers, we would be giving *them* a gift—of letting them have the pleasure of making a difference in their own unique way. That's something my sister taught me one summer.

Doctors told me to find someone to stay with me for a few days after having foot surgery because I wouldn't be able to walk. It was summer, and the first two people I asked had vacation plans. The third could come down during the day but couldn't stay overnight. The fourth could come if the surgery could be rescheduled. The fifth was my sister, who agreed to rearrange her family life—including kids, dogs, horses, job, and husband in Vermont—to be with me for forty-eight hours in Massachusetts.

There is no one I would rather have had helping me recover from surgery than my sister. She is an incredibly gifted nurse who knows a lot about pain and healing. At first, it was hard for me, her big sis, who had never needed to ask her for any help, to ask her to fix me something to eat or to get me an ice bag. Little things. I felt so helpless. Yet she said it was her pleasure to make me comfortable. She makes her living doing these sorts of things for complete strangers. What a difference it was, she said, for her to be able to do it for her only sister. I'd never thought about it that way.

Another thing that happened, because I "let" my sister help me, was that she got a break from her loving yet understandably demanding family. For the first time in years, she got to sit on a deck outside and read a book that wasn't for school or work but for the sheer pleasure of it. At one point out there on the deck, with books in our hands, we looked up and smiled at how lovely it was to share silence and be reading together like we did when we were kids. She also had time to herself to reflect on her busy life and to make some decisions about changing the way she and her family spend their time. Getting away from home to take care of me gave her a chance to think about taking better care of herself.

These moments with my sister were precious enough in themselves. However, I could have spoiled the joy she had in giving to me if I had tried to reciprocate right away. When people do things for you, it's not necessary to immediately do something for them. When you do that, you unintentionally take away their pleasure in having done something nice for you. It's fine to return a favor down the road. But when we immediately turn around and say to the person who's just helped us, "Now let me help you," it's usually because we feel a little too vulnerable, a little too close to someone. We shut down the "intimate" connection by trying to return the favor right away, rather than graciously accepting what has been given. Learning how to receive others' help is a gift in itself—to them and to us.

Just Listen

After a sudden loss

THE WARMTH OF HIS VOICE CAME THROUGH SOFTLY ON THE TELEPHONE. We hadn't seen each other in months. He had helped loosen the knots tied inside me after I'd been injured in several car crashes, forcing me to face up to the realities of my life.

He'd called today to apologize. "I'm so sorry," he said. "I told you I'd sent that report to your insurance company so you could be reimbursed for the massage therapy. Well, my wife had a miscarriage. She was typing the bills—it just never got sent."

"Darrel," I said, "this must be a difficult time. How old was the baby?"

"Eleven weeks," he said without pausing, almost surprised that I had said anything. "The doctors told us that the child had a lot of problems and, well, I guess God knew what he was doing.

"It's hard to believe," he continued. "When people at her office found out what had happened to my wife, they just avoided her. She came home the other day and said it was as if she had the plague. No one wanted to be around her. It's as if they don't know what to say, so they avoid her, and that's even worse."

"It must be hard for you to listen to your wife tell you that it's so uncomfortable for her at work when you had hoped her colleagues would understand," I said. "I'm wondering how this loss is affecting you, Darrel," I added, explaining that an old friend had taught me that the men who'd lost babies in miscarriages needed to talk, too. "He still mourns the loss, more than a decade later, of the son he never got to hold."

"Yes, yes," Darrel said, "people need to know this: just listen. Men need to talk, too."

Darrel's story reminds us that when friends or colleagues or family members are in a lot of pain in the early stages of a difficult situation, the kind of listening they want at this time is not for us to feel that we have to say a lot. However, if we sit there in pained silence, afraid to say anything, that won't be helpful either. It can be helpful to let them tell us what they're worried about. In the case of trying to heal after having a miscarriage, maybe they are scared of not being able to carry a child to term. They may be wondering whether it's a good idea to try again. It can be hard to resist trying to reassure them right away that there's an answer to the problem or a reason why they lost the baby. They may ask, "Why me?" It's a fair question. But we don't have to provide an answer. Instead, we can reflect back to them what it sounds like they are feeling through the words they are saying.

When your friend asks you, "Why me?" you could say, "Yes, it must be difficult not knowing why this happened." She might respond, "Yes, I feel that somehow it's my fault." You might then rephrase what she has told you by saying, "It sounds as if you would feel better if you could discover a reason why this happened." She might say, " I just don't understand. It's not fair." You might by now sense that she is angry, and if that's the case, very gently and without judging, offer an observation such as "It seems like you are angry." Then you would pause and she would either tell you that's the case or she might reveal another level of feeling by telling you, "No, I was angry at first, but now I'm just sad—very, very sad."

By paying attention to the words and to the energy you sense in their presence, you can let others know that you are being with them even if you can't know what it is like for them to go through this. By making it safe for them to feel whatever they are feeling and by letting them know that they don't need to chase those feelings away, they may then go on to tell you about the hopes they had for their child and the dreams they had for the little one they'd grown to love.

You can probably appreciate that not everyone who has had a miscarriage will want to talk about it right away. One person told me that her initial reaction to her miscarriage was "I didn't lose a baby; it was an eleven-week-old fetus." Years later, though, she realized that treating it like a medical condition, calling the child a fetus, had been her way of blocking the pain of loss and disappointment. It was years before she was able to tell anyone about the pain she'd been carrying around inside. This is why it's important to pay attention to the energy you feel as the conversation unfolds.

When people are going through difficult times, you can't always know, at first, whether they want to talk at all. Some may want to talk; others may feel that no one really wants to listen to them talk about how they feel. "After all," they think, "there's nothing anyone can do about it, so why bother?" However, when someone walks into your life who can make you feel that the only conversation important to them is the one they are having with you, that moment is a blessing.

Rediscovering Empathy

What comforts you may not comfort someone else

There were eight of us sitting around the lunch table. We were at a workshop where, sooner or later, we were supposed to talk about something we couldn't accomplish without asking for help. It was my turn to talk. I talked about wanting to write this book to help people help themselves and others through tough times. Times when they didn't know what to do or say. Without warning, Brian, the soft-spoken computer programmer in the group, said, "You mean like what to say to a kid when his sister is murdered?"

We all stopped eating. We'd known Brian for a couple of years. He'd married during the time our group had been coming to these professional development workshops in Atlanta. The workshops help you gain perspective on the past so that you can create a life based on your potential. We share personal stories. But none of us knew that when he was a boy, Brian's sister had been killed.

He didn't tell us the details. They weren't important. He did tell us something I will never forget. His voice got rough with quiet anger. His face showed a frown of remembered hurt. He asked me, "What do you think people want to learn?"

"What to say, or not to say, when someone's going through a difficult time," I explained.

Before I'd even finished my sentence, he jumped in, saying, "You mean like tell people not to pity you when someone dies?"

"Pity?" I asked.

"Yeah, pity," he said, almost spitting out the word. "You know, like when people try to tell you how bad they feel for your loss. I didn't need their pity. I wish they had just left me alone."

Suddenly there was a small cry, a stifled gasp. It came from his wife, Cheryl. They'd been married for about a year and had been going through the usual getting-to-know-you discoveries of newly married people. "That's why you leave me alone every time I get upset, isn't it?" she asked.

"Well, yes," Brian said. "I wouldn't want you to think I was sitting around feeling sorry for you. I leave because I think that what you want is some time for yourself."

"My God," she said, "you have confused empathy with pity. Back when you were a kid, people were trying to let you know how sad they were and that they felt bad, too. But you thought that they felt sorry for you or that you couldn't handle it."

Brian realized she was right. Whenever she was having a rough time, instead of putting his arms around the woman he loved and letting her know that he felt bad when she was upset, he would walk away, leaving her without the very comfort she needed. He told the group that sharing his story that day, so many years after his sister's death, had unexpectedly helped him heal an old wound and at the same time helped his marriage.

At one time or another, most of us have probably heard the phrase "Give what you want to receive." In this case, Brian gave his wife what he though she needed—time to be alone—because it was what he had thought he needed a long time ago when his world came crashing down around him. When his sister died, he wanted peace and quiet, not a lot of well-meaning people telling him how sorry they were. As a child, he couldn't know that what they were trying to do was comfort him. All he knew was that it felt like people pitied him.

Brian taught us an important lesson. When you are upset, no matter what your age, if a lot of people around you are saying how sorry they are, it can make you feel pitied. Since that day, I've tried to catch myself when I'm about to utter the often heard remark "I'm so sorry for your loss." I try to pause, and if I knew the person, say something like "I will miss John, too." If you can be specific about the loss, you can say something like "I can't believe this happened so suddenly—we had a wonderful time together just last week." Or briefly acknowledge the person's contribution to you, such as "Your father taught me . . . , and that has made a lasting difference in my life." Pausing to go beyond an automatic expression of condolence, even if it means you hesitate and feel awkward for a moment while you think of something to say, will be seen as a sincere effort on your part to take the time to connect with your heart rather than offer up a cliché.

If you don't know the person who has died, but you are a friend of the family, you can offer thoughts like "I can't imagine what it's like for you right now" or "I wish I had met your aunt Sarah. Sometime when you'd like to tell me about her, I'd love to hear some stories."

We are sculpted by our losses. The way we live through a loss can affect our relationships for a lifetime. In a single moment of sharing years of pent-up frustration, Brian helped his wife understand something very vital. He didn't walk away from her in times of pain because he didn't care. He was trying to give her what he thought she needed based on his own life experiences.

We grow up in different families and different cultures and have different ways of experiencing loss. When we're upset, we can easily forget that there may be good reasons why certain people don't seem to be there for us. It's never too late to appreciate people's best intentions by learning more about the life experiences that led them to try to comfort us in the ways that they did. For example, in certain cultures, people raise their voices to show passion, not anger. Tears aren't allowed in some families, who view crying as a sign of weakness. And some families subscribe to the same motto no matter what the problem: "Just *deal* with it!"

Sometimes cultural differences have nothing to do with not getting what we need. Maybe, as Cheryl discovered that day, we weren't very clear about asking for what we needed—we assumed that the other just knew. "Missed understandings" are a rich opportunity for us to go beyond our assumptions of one another—to discover there may be a poignantly rich reason why we see the world and express our needs differently. What Brian learned was that his wife didn't need him to say anything when she was upset; all she wanted was to be gently held.

It'll Be OK, Sugarplum

Being a light at the end of the tunnel

Every Monday I could count on it being there. No matter where I was in the country, no matter what was going on in his family's life, it would be there. The voice. The message. It went something like this: "Hey, darlin'. Just wanted you to know we're thinking of you wherever you are. We know things look pretty rough right now, but there is a light at the end of the tunnel, and we know you'll get through to the other side someday. We just know it. It'll be OK, Sugarplum."

Almost every week during one of the most confusing times of my life, I'd get this message on my voice mail. It came from my friend and business partner, Logan, and sometimes from his wife, Rhonda. It was a vigil that they kept up for a year. Sometimes when they were going away on holiday, they'd call and leave a message before they left, just so I'd know they still cared. Logan told me that when Rhonda was a little girl growing up in New Orleans, her grandfather used to reassure her by saying, "It'll be OK, Sugarplum."

What's the big deal, you might ask, about an innocuous phrase like that?

Well, when you aren't sure whether or not you are going to go through with a divorce, aren't sure you can make a living on your own because you feel so burned out, and are beating yourself up in a series of intense personal growth workshops on the meaning of your life . . . when you move around the country from one consulting client to another, living in hotels, dorms, and clients' guest rooms . . . well, you can lose your compass. That's it. Those messages were like a compass that I could tune in to each week and know, in that moment, that I was loved.

When friends are having a rough time, sometimes all they need is for you to check in. No advice. Just sincere encouragement. Some perspective that maybe things will work out. You aren't telling them to see the glass as half full. You aren't telling them to "think positive." Your message isn't just in the words. It's in the energy behind the words.

When Logan and Rhonda left those messages, the energy behind their words was that they had faith in me. They didn't make me feel that just because I couldn't get my life completely together, I was falling apart. They didn't try to fix me, either. Instead, they were giving me grace—permission— to be in the messy place that I was in while also acknowledging that I had very little faith in much of anything. They didn't try to talk me into or out of my feelings. They believed that somehow I would make it because they had faith in me and in the universe. Their messages came like clockwork. They were a small "care package." Sometimes that's all we can offer. Sometimes it is enough.

Mommy, Will He Be OK?

Helping children face their fears **and** *yours*

WHAT DO YOU SAY TO A CHILD WHEN SHE SEES THAT A BELOVED ANIMAL IS ill or dying and asks, "Mommy, will he be OK?" That's what my friend Anne faced one weekend when the horse she had just bought for her oldest daughter, Jill, had a brush with death. Anne's story unfolded in an e-mail late one night.

It's Sunday evening, and the last three days at home have been extremely stressful and traumatic. Where to begin to tell you about our family's life and near-death experience on Thursday?

Thursday afternoon I was working at our little hospital after being on call until midnight on Wednesday. I was tired but looking forward to being relieved a bit early and heading over to the barn to watch Jill have a late-afternoon training session on her new horse, Sage. But around 3 P.M., Henry [her husband] called, his voice shaky and frightened. He said, "We have a crisis at the barn. Sage has colic and it's bad."

The barn manager had called Henry around 11 to tell him that Sage was sick and that he and Jill should come to the barn right away. You may not know this, but colic is a life-threatening kind of indigestion that a horse can get for lots of different reasons. Unless you can get the intestines to untwist by themselves, the horse needs surgery or a decision has to be made to put him down.

The vet had already been called. At first, he tried the standard conservative treatment—keep the horse walking to see if the intestines will become unblocked on their own. For hours, Jill walked and walked Sage around the indoor arena. When Henry tried to take her place to give her a break, Sage wouldn't budge. The horse would walk in pain, but only for Jill.

By the time I arrived at the barn, Sage was in critical condition. He was in a cold sweat, no longer able to move around. His eyes were full of fear and pain. It was an intensely emotional moment for me, arriving at the barn where just 24 hours earlier Jill had enjoyed her first training session on her new horse. Now I joined her in the stall, both of us sobbing and scared. Jill asked me, "Mommy, is he going to be OK?"

All I could say to her at that moment was, "Honey, I don't know."

When, in becoming a parent, do we learn how to tell our children for the first time that no, it may not be OK?

With the minutes flying by, we decided to take Sage to surgery and hope the obstruction was repairable. Would he be able to jump again? Would he live with pain? Would he face this nightmare again? After two years of tremendous effort in searching for Jill's first horse, why is she faced with such heartbreak so young, so soon?

Henry, Jill, and the vet loaded Sage onto the trailer and took off for the hospital. Diane [her younger daughter] and I followed behind in the car, spending the 45-minute drive to the hospital in and out of tears—no music, no conversation, just a silent shared misery. When we arrived, they were preparing Sage for the operation. The vet invited us to watch the operation. I was amazed and initially declined. Henry went into the operating room first. Later, he came back to the waiting room to tell us that Sage looked like a big puppy lying on its back, legs in the air as if to say please scratch my belly. Then a very brave Diane went in with her daddy and they watched together. Jill and I now sat on the window seat. Holding my hand, she again asked, "Sage is gonna be all right, isn't he, Mommy?" This time she didn't look at me, just lay her face on the pillow, cheeks red and tear streaked, her hand warm and tight in mine. I couldn't answer her. Instead I looked out the window beyond the sunset as if I might find an answer deep in the mountains surrounding us.

Before I could find a way to answer my daughter's question, Dr. Forbes exclaimed, "Wow, look at this! I can fix it!" Curiosity overcame my fear of seeing Sage anesthetized, and I went into the operating room with Jill still holding my hand. It is excruciating for me to be in the presence of animals in pain, knowing that I can't explain to them why they are suffering. It was truly an amazing moment, to be standing side by side with my daughters and husband in that operating room, watching Dr. Forbes untangle and reposition Sage's intestines.

On Friday we all went to visit Sage. Less than 24 hours out from his surgery, he was up, eager to walk with Jill, and equally eager to eat. We couldn't feed him today, but Jill brushed all the dried blood off and then gave him a sponge bath. It was a special moment seeing the two of them so strong together. These animals are miracles in our midst, and it will be interesting, years from now, to hear Jill and Diane recount their memories of this time we shared in crisis and recovery.

I am so touched by the purity of a child's belief that everything will be all right. Having faced the threat of death for the first time, the girls simply asked what we needed to do to help Sage get better. A child's untarnished hope is beautiful to see.

What do we say to children in the midst of their first life-and-death situation? Do we show them our fear and our pain? How do we answer their questions when we don't have any answers ourselves? Those were some of the questions I asked Anne a few weeks after she had helped her family navigate this trauma. She told me that during her nursing career in intensive care, she had spent many hours with children and their families. She had come to appreciate that whereas adults often want to know all the details of what is wrong and what will happen, children are different. In her experience, it's important to give youngsters just as much information as they need but not overwhelm them with more than they can comprehend. "You learn to go slow and let them ask the questions," she explained.

"I've also learned that children have a right to know how we—their parents—are doing," Anne admitted. "Sometimes it is so tempting to keep our own feelings bottled up inside in our attempts to make a child think everything is going to be OK. But we underestimate children when we do that. They are very sensitive to our energy, and although they may not know exactly what we are keeping from them, they know something isn't quite right. That's why when my daughter asked whether her horse would be OK, I told her honestly that I didn't know. It was the truth. I wanted to look her in the eyes and tell her everything would be OK. What mother wouldn't want to reassure her child in this way? But I knew I owed her the truth: I was hopeful, but I was also scared. Sharing my own fears made it possible for her to let me know how frightened she was, and then we could comfort each other."*

"What would you have done if you had been told by the doctor that there was nothing he could do to save the horse's life?" I asked.

"I would have explained to the girls that Sage was in a lot of pain and that our veterinarian could not operate on him. Then I would reassure them that when an animal is in this much pain and the vet cannot fix it, he can stop the pain by euthanizing the animal. Of course, I would explain that this is an act of compassion and kindness. Most of all in facing this crisis, I would have made sure that the girls had the chance to say goodbye. I know that when we don't get that chance to say goodbye—to a beloved pet or person—the death doesn't seem real, and it may take longer to come to terms with the loss. Sometimes we never do."

If we let children see that like them, we are hurting and scared, we provide them with the reassurance that what they are feeling is OK; it's part of being human. When we hide our pain or our fears, we teach our children to do the same. We make it harder for them to ask for help and for us to know what they need—not only when they are children but perhaps throughout their lives.

*Experts caution parents, however, not to overload a child by sharing too much in the way of raw emotions, especially if a parent is greatly upset and hasn't had a chance to gain perspective.

Asking One Friend to Help Another
🐚 *When you don't have the answers*

WHAT DO YOU DO WHEN A FRIEND CALLS, ASKING FOR HELP, AND INITIALLY you have no idea of how to provide it? There are days when we may need to ask another friend to help out instead of us doing it ourselves.

I never knew what chemotherapy was really like until a friend called to tell me that she was having a hard time with her treatment. "No one told me it would be this rough," she said in a voice that barely carried over the phone. "It feels as if the life is being sucked out of my body—as if I am being drained of everything. I can't sleep, my thoughts are fuzzy, and I can't hold down any food. Everything I eat makes me nauseous, and the antinausea medication has horrible side effects. I'm down to eighty-seven pounds, and no one seems to know what to do to help me."

"I don't know what to tell you," I said. "I've heard about how bad chemo can be, but I don't know what to say to help you right now. It sounds like your

doctors have done what they can and that what you need is to talk to someone who has been through chemo and come out on the other side. Let me
think about who I can call, and I'll get back to you."

Then I thought about whether I could actually call the person who might
be able to help my friend. I'd have to be sensitive with this request because
my friend Richard was never willing to talk to me about his experiences with
chemo. He made it clear, years ago when he was battling lymphoma, that talking about his treatment wasn't something he wanted to do. "Talk about anything else," he'd say firmly. But today could be different. He's healthy, in
remission, and living the life of someone who had cancer and beat it. Would
he be willing to talk about it now?

I left him a message explaining that a friend needed his help. "Would you
be willing to give her some tips on how to get through chemotherapy for a
cancer she has been told is incurable? The doctors are trying some experimental treatments, hoping for a breakthrough or hoping to at least prolong
her life. She's been on a strict, mostly vegetarian diet. She has a meditation
coach working with her. She's overwhelmed by the nausea and is puzzled
about why she is craving foods she banned from her diet over a year ago—
foods like french fries and ice cream. Can you help her handle any of this?"

Richard wrote her a wonderful e-mail, urging her to take control of her
life so that chemotherapy wouldn't take control of her. He was not trying to
be a medical expert on dealing with chemo; he was just reflecting his experiences. What he offered my friend, whom he'd never met, was not only information but also a way of not feeling quite so alone.

❧ Although having a positive mind is a very important thing, and
meditation and relaxation help, it can only work if the body is doing

something right, too. All the meditation won't help if you are uncomfortable all the time and you cannot see a window through the tunnel. I spent many hours lying on the couch and feeling miserable, but I realized there would be three or four days where I would be feeling good, and then it was back to the miserable cycle of chemotherapy and nausea and diarrhea and listlessness and weakness. I knew there would be some "good days," so I focused on that. You have to move around. Don't stay sedentary, because the body is fighting the cancer and the chemo. In fact, I used to get up off the couch and walk a path around the apartment, like a little walking track.

Go ahead and have a hamburger with fries and ketchup, or a vanilla milkshake, or pizza and anything you like, and enjoy it. Don't overdo it, but these foods, though full of fat, are what your body needs to bulk up a bit and absorb some protein and carbohydrates and fatty acids and everything else.* If you don't give your body some fuel to work with, it gets worse.

I believe that in certain cases, some condition that's said to be incurable is actually curable. It may be incurable today, but until you explore each and every option, it may ultimately be curable. And frankly, if the inevitable is that you know when the end is going to happen, then live it up. Do whatever the hell you want to do. At least you have the option of knowing. But damn it, fight, strategize, seek information, and do anything you can.

---

*This advice is not based on medical opinion. The approach helped Richard, and his sharing it helped my friend understand her cravings and not feel so alone.

Richard then offered her a meditation scenario that, when I read it, helped me understand how important it is to offer someone a sense of hope and, if possible, to do it with a sense of humor. It was a meditative process he came up with on his own one day during his chemotherapy treatments that initially felt anything but healing.

🕊️ As you lie there, don't think about anything else; just empty yourself of everything. Your stomach may hurt, and your little veins in the top of your hands may be tingling—from the chemo needles—or you may feel weak, or you may feel nauseous, or you may feel fine. It takes some time to unconsciously get into this "empty" state. Try to think only about your body, not your situation, just your body and your breathing.

Now here's the tricky part. Once you've relaxed, picture some things in your mind. This can be fun! My favorite was to picture a bunch of big men in white plastic suits, lined up like they're in the army, carrying all kinds of tools—huge drills and cranes and explosives and jackhammers and picks and stuff. They are fighting men. And they were in my body, in the "tunnels" of my bloodstream, hammering and chipping away and beating up at the guys in black, who were the "bad cancer" guys eating mouthfuls of my blood cells. But there were far more white-plastic-suited guys outnumbering the black-suited guys, and the white-suited guys were always winning. They would hammer away and I would breathe and picture 10,000 of these good guys attacking 1,000 of the bad guys. It was wonderful. My breathing would slow down, and I could feel the soreness from the effects of chemo, and I was a little nauseous. Then it would go away temporarily.

Then, at some point, and this is magical, I would take a nap! This is a huge secret: take naps! Take a nap whenever you want, because the body is going through this battle against the chemo and this battle with the toxic avengers and with the attacking cancer cells. Be strong. Try everything.

Richard, like many cancer patients, is fiercely private about his experiences with the disease. He didn't tell many people when he was diagnosed years ago, and he hasn't told many people since being in remission. That's why I was reluctant to ask for his help. Thank goodness I did. Not only was he able to help my friend, but he was also able to open up to us about an experience that took remarkable courage, a sense of humor, and creativity—not just to survive but also to thrive. Retelling his stories to my friend made him realize that what he had endured had value—that it was worth giving up a limited amount of his privacy to help someone else.

Sometimes you simply aren't the one who can help a friend who asks. But you might be able to build a bridge of comfort between two people who start out as strangers but then travel wherever they need to go to help each other on their journey.

Unexpected Gifts

Accepting help from a stranger

THREE WOMEN ARE STANDING IN LINE WAITING TO ORDER AT ONE OF THOSE fashionable upscale restaurants where you can get fabulous French cooking at a cafeteria bistro. Out of the blue, a gentleman comes up and says to one of them, the tall, elegant, soft-spoken, sparkly-eyed blonde, "Excuse me, I just have to tell you, you are so beautiful." Then he walks away.

The other two ladies are delighted. They giggle and stifle a whoop because they've been telling their friend for years how beautiful she is. But Elisabeth doesn't believe them. She discounts their compliments and sees herself as not particularly attractive. Her reaction to the man's attention was to blush and to be embarrassed.

They're again standing in line waiting to pick up their orders when the guy comes back and says the same thing to Elisabeth: "I just have to tell you again, you are *soooo* beautiful." And he walks away.

By now Elisabeth is really embarrassed. She went out today without even putting on any makeup—not something that a well-trained southern woman ordinarily does. But today isn't an ordinary day. Putting on her face wasn't high on her to-do list this morning when she took Ron, her beloved husband of thirty-three years, for his first chemotherapy treatment. The supposedly benign tumor he'd had removed the month before had, to their astonishment, turned out to be cancerous, and everything had changed.

Today she is with her best buddies for some moral support after having been with her husband at the hospital. It was a ladies' lunch break. And during the lunch they finally are eating, the same guy shows up a third time. Only this time he doesn't walk away. He wants to make sure that this beautiful woman doesn't think he is trying to hit on her. Flirt maybe, but that wasn't even the point of his comments to her. He explains himself in a way that suddenly makes each of the wary women give him their complete attention.

"You see," he tells them, "I've been diagnosed with an inoperable brain tumor. It has spread everywhere, and I don't have long to live. These days, I just say what I want, when I want. And you are beautiful, and I wanted you to know it. I'm sorry if I've embarrassed you, but life is so short, and I wasn't going to sit there and ignore what my heart told me to say."

Each of the women has tears in her eyes as he speaks his truth to them. Slowly Elisabeth starts telling her story to this man, who moments ago had been a stranger she was afraid of and was ready to avoid. She tells him about her husband. About their determination to fight the colon cancer. As luck, fate, or more than coincidence would have it, this stranger is a doctor, a brain surgeon. Upon hearing her story, he pauses to acknowledge that his mind is working a little slower these days, as he gropes for the name and number of the cancer specialist he wants to give her. Eventually he remembers it, writes it down, and hands her what could be a lifeline in her husband's battle.

The funny thing is that just a week earlier, this attractive, loving wife had told her friends that she was going to try living more in the present. She wanted to be less concerned about the future. To be less concerned about what people would think of her taking a leave of absence from her "very important" job to help her husband through this treatment. She wanted to see what life would be like if she just paid attention to the little moments, to the present.

Look what showed up on her plate at lunch with friends! Had she slipped into embarrassed avoidance or annoyed judgment, she might have driven away the gift of a dying man's determination to live his life, one beautiful moment at a time. Appreciating the unexpected takes practice. It takes a willingness to suspend judgment of another's motives and an openness to be with what is. Being with what is takes practice because it doesn't necessarily come naturally. Of course, you can exercise common sense and make sure your gut tells you the situation is safe. And if that's the case, then you can take a step toward being open, which means letting yourself be curious about what someone you don't know, who owes you nothing, is trying to give you for no apparent reason.

When things aren't going the way you'd planned in life, you definitely need your friends. You need to be able to laugh and to cry and to wonder why life has taken an unexpected turn. Sometimes, though, a stranger does come into your life—at a restaurant, on an airplane, in a hospital waiting room— and that stranger can offer you an extraordinary gift if you have the presence of mind and heart to be open to receiving it.

Before *and* After the Move

🖎 *Emotional attics and new road maps*

WHEN FRIENDS OR FAMILY MOVE AWAY, THERE'S A LOT WE CAN DO TO HELP. But sometimes it's not what we do that is most helpful. Everyone knows that moving is stressful. What some of us may not know, until we go through it ourselves, is that a lot of the stress of moving is about feeling like you don't have enough emotional room to make way for the memories.

Pat and Jim were close friends who had a few weeks left before the moving trucks came. They were moving out of the dream home they'd lived in for ten years just before they retired. Late one afternoon, I called to see how things were going with the packing. I wasn't sure what I could do to help.

"We have so much *stuff!*" Pat moaned. "I'm trying to put things into piles: 'keep,' 'give to the kids,' 'give to charity,' 'sell,' 'take to the dump,' and 'don't know what to do with.' I'm having trouble getting rid of stuff I know I won't need anymore but is hard for me to give up."

She went on to talk about her memories. Memories attached to a particular outfit of clothes, pictures, keepsakes—and then there were the unexpected discoveries of things that had belonged to her mom. Things that when her mom had died three years ago, she had put away in a box to go through later. "What am I supposed to do with my dad's first paycheck?" she asked. "When I came across it in the box, I started realizing just how much Mum had to cope with bringing us up with so little money. She never remarried after my dad died—it was New Year's Eve; he was hit by a passing car while changing a tire at the side of the road. This old pay stub, from before I was born, reminds me of how little he made back then and how hard Mum had to work to get by after he died—there's this flood of memories. I don't need that piece of paper, and yet it's part of our family's history, though I'm not sure it means anything to anyone else. It's hard to know what to do with these treasures."

At this point I didn't know whether Pat needed to keep talking about how scared she was or whether she was asking for help in deciding what to do about family treasures. It wasn't clear to me, so I asked her if it would be helpful to hear about a method I'd stumbled across that helped me when I'd moved.

"Yes," she said. "I'd love to hear about another way of getting through this."

"After sifting through four generations of family stuff, here's what I learned the last time I moved," I explained. "When I took the time to appreciate the role something had played in my life and then I let it go, I have never regretted what I've given up. However, when I got tired, overwhelmed, or out of time and started just 'getting rid of stuff,' months or years later, those were the things I felt I hadn't gotten rid of at all. They still had a hold on me even though I had sold them or given them away or donated them to charity. That is when I learned that there's a difference between getting rid of things and letting them go."

Pat told me that this idea helped her see how to let go of things instead of making herself feel wrong for having so much. "I feel lighter already," she added. "There's just one thing, however. I'm realizing that I'm scared about not knowing what I'll need in the future. The other day I was trying to get rid of the kinds of clothes I don't think I'll need anymore now that I'm retiring. What I've remembered is that when Mum was bringing us up, after Dad died, I was given some dresses by our school janitor's family. I guess maybe the reason it's hard for me to get rid of the clothes I have bought for myself is that I'm not sure whether in the future, without a salary, I'll still be able to buy the things I'll need."

"So it's a matter of faith," I said rephrasing what I sensed was behind her words. "You're saying that you want to have faith that you will be able to generate what you will need in your new life."

"I'd never thought of it that way," she replied. "Here I've been imagining the worst and not remembering how much I've learned to earn my way, stretch a dollar, go without, buy bargains, and still enjoy it all. I'd forgotten and been worrying about not having enough when right now I feel bad about having too much."

When people move, there are a great many unknowns. Friends and family need to talk about what they'll miss and what they're worried about. Pat didn't realize what was bothering her until the end of our conversation. That's when she understood that it wasn't all the stuff she'd collected that was weighing her down. Having depended on the charity of others when she was a child, she was worried that in retirement, without an income, she might not be able to afford the things she needed. When we began speaking, she was more over-whelmed by the task of sorting things. By the time we ended our conversation, she had sorted through her feelings and memories. It takes time to let friends and family walk us through their emotional attics, where they've stored so much for so long.

After the move, friends and family need our support and more. Resettling can be *unsettling* in ways that aren't always obvious to us. There are plenty of times when people feel lost in their new environment. It's not the kind of lost where they can't find their way around with a map. It's the kind of lost where they can't get their emotional bearings.

If you're like most people who move, you knew where to find things in your old house and your old neighborhood. You knew the rhythms of the traffic, the birds, and the weather. You knew who you could count on in an emergency—friends, a spiritual or religious community, a neighbor. You knew the best grocery store, were on a first-name basis with the pharmacist, knew which gas station had a good mechanic, and knew the best escape routes to take when highways were jammed. In the old neighborhood, there were smiles for you in places where you forget they matter: the post office, the bank, the hardware store. In your new town, you're the stranger who doesn't belong—yet.

How can you support people who have moved to a new town and feel out of place?

- Tell them the commuting shortcuts and your favorite back roads.
- Call them when the first storm hits to see how they are managing; better yet, call them before it hits to see if you can help them prepare.
- See if they need help finding a plumber, a doctor, a babysitter—give them the inside scoop on who has a good reputation in your area.

- And if you are one of those friends left behind in the old neighborhood, don't be a stranger; call every once in a while to see how they are adjusting.

It can take years to grieve quietly over what you miss from your former home, whether it's the trees you planted or playing with the neighbor's dog. When friends and family move, it may seem to you (and them) that all they have done is move to a different dot on a map. But it takes more than a road map to help them find their way.

It's Not What You Think

The hidden hurts of bankruptcy

FEW OF US THINK WE KNOW ANYONE WHO HAS GONE BANKRUPT. ONE REA-son may be that it's not something many people feel they can safely talk about without being judged. So we don't know that it has happened to them. People go bankrupt for different reasons, including high medical bills in the wake of an accident or catastrophic illness, something that went terribly wrong with a business, overspending, or betrayal. Regardless of the reason, it is important to be sensitive to the realities a family faces during the years it takes to recover.

"I never thought it could happen to people like us," Andrea said, talking about what it was like when she and her husband, Peter, had to declare both personal and business bankruptcy. "One thing that was difficult was that some of our friends didn't want to be around us because they thought, 'If it can happen to them, it could happen to me.'

> One day we were owners of a successful company that employed fifty-six people. We'd always met payroll. Always paid our suppliers

on time. We worked twelve-hour days and loved it. Our employees were like family, and our customers could depend on us. Suddenly, the IRS called to say it had seized our assets and we had forty-eight hours to pay $150,000 in back taxes.

We didn't know what had hit us. It was twenty-four hours of being in shock—like having someone punch you in the stomach and you can't breathe or even think. Then we had to go into action using our savings to pay employees one day and then letting half of them go the next day. Only later did we discover that the reason we went bankrupt was that money had been embezzled from the company. But by that time it was too late and we were in bankruptcy proceedings.

One of the most awful moments was seeing our equipment— about $750,000 worth of items that we'd worked hard to buy—sold. We were assured by the bankruptcy lawyer that it would be sold at a public auction. But for whatever reason it was sold privately to an individual for $25,000. There was no auction! Shortly after our equipment was sold, that individual resold most of it for $160,000. Had we been allowed to sell it ourselves, rather than the bankruptcy manager, we could have done much better. But once you declare bankruptcy, you are no longer in charge of anything.

At the same time that we realized we were no longer in charge of our life, we also realized something else: now that we weren't owners of a company, we weren't even employed! We also felt like we'd lost our identity. All of this personal turmoil was going on behind the scenes of trying to find some way to pay our suppliers, pay the rent, and buy groceries.

"What did people do to help you get through those early days?" I asked Andrea.

🐾 One friend just let me talk about how horrified I was. How angry I was about how we were being treated by the bankruptcy officials. How I didn't know what we had done wrong. How ashamed we felt. I also talked about how awful it was to feel like a victim . . . how awful that someone would embezzle from us and then *we'd* have to pay the ultimate price. The most important thing was that my friend didn't try to commiserate with me about how terrible it was. Once I got to say what I was thinking, I was able to begin to get some perspective. Somehow my friend knew that's what I needed and didn't try to give me solutions or even make me feel that it wasn't all my fault.

Then Andrea explained that in the early days of the bankruptcy, there were weeks when she and her husband didn't know where they'd get the money to buy groceries for their family. She had two teenagers at the time. "Did anyone offer to loan you money?" I asked, wondering whether it would be helpful or offensive to make this kind of gesture to someone in her situation.

🐾 Several people told us, "If there is anything we can do, please ask." So we did ask one friend for a loan of $10,000, and that helped us catch our breath so that we could figure out how to live through what was to be a long process we were totally unprepared to manage. That's the other thing that your friends need to know when you are going through a bankruptcy process. There is no support group. You aren't prepared for how you will be treated by the bankruptcy officials. I realize that some people misuse the bankruptcy process and take advantage of it unfairly, and maybe that's why the officials are so strict. However, we weren't prepared to be treated like criminals, and at times that's how it felt.

As fate would have it, I spoke to Andrea the day before Thanksgiving. It had been three years ago at Thanksgiving that she and her husband had moved away from their hometown, trying to get a fresh start.

> ❧ It's been five years since we went bankrupt, and you know what the hardest thing is today? It's not the embarrassment about when you go to get a loan. It's not the process we went through to redis-cover who we were if we weren't business owners. It's not even the friends we lost along the way. It's that on the outside, to everyone else, our life looks fine. We have food for Thanksgiving. We have a home. My husband has a new job. But the hardest thing is that oth-ers can't see what's still going on inside of you. The hardest thing years later is walking into a Wal-Mart and thinking, "I can't afford to buy a pair of jeans even at a discount." It's not that I don't have the money. It's that I will always be thinking that if I spend it today, I may not have enough when I least expect that I'll need it. It's the panic one of us feels when we worry about whether it could happen again.

What else do we need to be sensitive to when trying to support someone who is going through or has experienced a bankruptcy? We can avoid jump-ing to conclusions about what caused the financial crisis. In the words of Mary Kay, another friend who went through bankruptcy, "My advice? Don't assume that because someone still has a nice car or a nice house or a child who gets married that you know the whole story. I can't tell you how much it hurt to learn how friends were saying things behind our back. Shortly after we unexpectedly went bankrupt, our child got married and we had a live band at the wedding. We heard that people were wondering how we could afford it. What I wanted to say to people, but of course didn't, was that the music at the wedding was a gift from a dear friend."

Friends need to know that we value them regardless of their possessions or position in life. We can have compassion for them years later when they try to get a loan or to be approved by a credit bureau, knowing that their financial past may still be an unseen albatross. Perhaps what is most valued by someone who is dealing with bankruptcy isn't what we say at all. It's that we set aside our assumptions and judgments.

Who Am I If I'm Not Who I Was?

🙢 *After a life-changing event*

THERE ARE TIMES WHEN A DIAGNOSIS, AN ACCIDENT, THE LOSS OF A JOB, OR the end of a marriage can rob you of your identity. Suddenly, you are no longer the person you thought you were or would live out your life to become. What do you say when friends, colleagues, or family members wake up to discover that they don't know who they are anymore? Barbara offers us lessons in supporting others when they hit that wall of fear.

The message Barbara left on her friend's voice mail was this: "I'm calling to let you know that I got some bad news today. It wasn't a surprise, but it wasn't what I was hoping for, either. I'm not sure how to take the news. I'm trying to let it sink in. The cancer is back. Tests showed there are more malignancies. I'm not sure what I can do. I have a lot to think about. I'd like to talk."

When the friend returned the call, she asked Barbara, "What's going on?"

"It's back," she said simply. "There are cancer cells showing up as small tumors. I'm not surprised—we knew this could happen—but I've been so healthy! I look and feel better than before the cancer. Part of me can't believe this is happening. I thought maybe I'd beaten it. I've been feeling so well, I just can't believe it."

Then she went on to explain in a waterfall of words: "I can't stop thinking about this question: Who am I, if I can't be the person I have been? Who am I, a former travel company CEO, if I'm not running a company? What if I don't have my energy, my exuberance? What will I be if I can't get around and am lying in a bed for months? I've never been like that; I just can't imagine it. I'm scared to even think about it."

What could you say to a friend who told you she felt this lost? How might you help her rediscover that her ability to make a difference is still there? That it may just express itself in new ways? How would you help your friend put the pieces of her life together bit by bit even though at this moment she is feeling disoriented?

Barbara's friend paused because for a moment she wasn't sure what to say. She had to think back about the many things Barbara had told her. She had to get her own bearings before helping Barbara find her way. Barbara sounded as if she was in shock over the cancer returning in spite of her best efforts to beat it. Barbara had also talked about losing her identity. Who she was had been wrapped up, as for so many of us, in her career. What did her friend really need from her right now, especially since there was nothing she could say to make the cancer go away? Barbara had been holding on to the hope of being able to somehow run her life again, the way she had before the cancer, and now suddenly all of that had changed.

"You seem to be afraid of not having a set of goals or purpose in your life like you did when you were a CEO," her friend observed, rephrasing some of the concerns Barbara had expressed. "It also sounds like you are looking for some new way to see yourself living in the future. Would you like some help creating a new picture of who you could possibly become?"

"That's it!" Barbara cried. "I'm looking for some perspective. Please help me find a new way to see things because right now I can't even think straight!"

"Well, since you've asked, here's the picture I see," her friend said. "Barbara, a year ago, if I'd told you that in the next twelve months, you would become a strict vegetarian and inspire others to clean up their health; that you would have a busy, fulfilling life even after giving up a management job you loved and couldn't imagine living without; that you would take vacation after vacation and go places with people you truly enjoyed; that you'd learn how to let people help you; that you'd put together an extraordinary relationship with your ex-husband; that you—an extremely private person—would get involved in publicly telling your story and counseling others; that doctors across New York City would call you their star patient, recovering from major abdominal cancer surgery faster than anyone on record; and that you'd forge a worldwide network of cancer specialists in both the medical and alternative healing communities, you would have said, 'You're out of your mind.'"

"You're right," Barbara laughed. "It's amazing to hear how much I've learned in spite of all of the pain, frustration, and fear. I don't think I could have added it all up quite that way. Thank you for reminding me of where I've been and all the people who've contributed to me. It's really extraordinary."

At this point, what would you do to help your friend reframe the picture of her life? How could you help her shift from seeing her life and purpose from what they had been to what they could become in the near future? How might you help your friend get the fears out of her head and into the daylight?

Barbara's friend suggested that she take a practical approach to addressing her fears. "Today you're telling me you can't imagine who you will become if you can't travel or be full of energy. OK, so what about writing down on a piece of paper all the things you are afraid of? Ask yourself, 'What's the worst that could happen?' There's nothing wrong with fear unless you don't have the courage to admit feeling it. Fear helps you know what's important and what's not important. So get it all out there, out of the whirlpool of your mind."

"I never thought of it like that," Barbara said with a chuckle. "You're right. I never would have thought that I could go from CEO to no job and wind up with a whole new life that is more full of life than I could have ever planned. I never thought I'd get my figure back after the surgery, let alone look better than I had before. I never thought I'd take an ad out in a magazine, for goodness sake, and ask, 'Is there anyone out there like me?' I never thought I'd learn to let people help me or depend on them and learn to enjoy it. I never thought I'd be the person I am today because I couldn't imagine not being who I was."

How do we give others perspective when they are feeling panic? We remind them about how they have hurdled obstacles to get this far in their life. We acknowledge what they have learned along the way. We don't minimize what they are facing. We do remind them of what they have overcome so far.

In Barbara's case, she was afraid that she didn't know what she would do with herself if she didn't have a job, responsibilities, or her CEO identity. By asking herself what was the worst that could happen if she lost all that, she realized that she could use all her business skills to mobilize resources to treat her cancer, conduct research for new treatments, and educate others. She realized that after losing one purpose, she could create a new one, but only after being able to safely write down what she was most afraid of—losing her identity.

It's Over

❧ *A relationship ends*

WHEN A RELATIONSHIP ENDS, LOTS OF PEOPLE TRY TO MAKE YOU FEEL BETter by saying things like "It's not about you; it's about him. Don't beat up on yourself" or "You'll see, there's someone even better out there for you" or "It's better to have loved and lost than not to have loved at all" or "I knew she wasn't right for you. You deserve better."

The trouble is that you probably don't need to hear any of these phrases hours or days after a relationship ends. You need to rant, rave, be down on yourself, wonder what the heck happened again, forswear relationships forever—you need someone who can listen to you be irrational, angry, sad, irritable, frustrated, and messy. You don't need people telling you their story. You don't need friends or relatives to tell you they know how you feel; they don't. The challenge for a friend in this situation is sitting through the early phase of someone's painful breakup.

When a relationship ended abruptly, I turned to some friends for insights into what had gone wrong. When my friend David called, he broke through all the advice-giving clamor I'd heard from other friends to say instead, "I know it hurts. And all your attempts to try to figure this out and understand it won't make the hurt go away." Later he encouraged me not to try to be someone I wasn't and to stop worrying about changing how I was in a relationship. He told me that only when he was able to accept himself as he was, to stop trying to be what others thought they wanted him to be—only then could he relax enough to stop feeling angry or bottled up. His comments helped me because I had been driving myself nuts listening to people give me advice about how I had to change.

In an e-mail to my friend Andy Fleming, I wrote about the frustration I was feeling about people plying me with well-meaning platitudes. He wrote about his own experience that same weekend, when of all the people at the daylong Outward Bound ropes course, he was the only one who hadn't made it up the course; he had backed down the ladder. It drove him nuts when everyone tried to make him feel better about chickening out. After all, he's six foot seven and has always been an athlete; if anyone could make it on the ropes course, he thought, it should have been him.

All he wanted to do was to be upset about it, but no one wanted him to be upset. That's the problem right there. Too few of us, myself included, know much about how to be with someone who is sad, angry, or confused. I'm not talking about being with someone who feels threatening. I mean being with someone in the sense of not trying to make it all better right away.

During our e-mail correspondence about how frustrating it was to deal with our friends' well-intentioned counsel, Andy wrote a poem. He's given me permission to print it here; it has since been published in a longer version in his book, *Backing Down the Ladder.*

NOTHING IS REQUIRED

Let us share a moment of little faith,
the minister said,
or no faith at all
if that's where you are.
All that I can say
is that nothing
is required of you
this moment here right now . . .
no doing
no thinking
no spiritual jujitsu
to see the blessing in your fears and tears . . .
nothing is required of you today.
Let us join hands
and sing hymns
to life's holy incompleteness.

It's hard to know what to say to someone who's angry about a broken relationship or who is embarrassed about something that didn't work out. In the early days or hours after the initial "it's over" event, your friend may be reliving moments from previous times when he or she felt hurt or disappointed. The loss of a relationship is a lot like the loss we experience around the death of someone. That's why your friend may recall memories of every other loss—from the loss of a pet to the loss of a parent, friend, or teacher—and of course other intimate relationships that have ended. Your friend may need you to be a safe space for recalling those memories, whether they are bitter or have softened with time.

As your friend comes to terms with the end of a relationship, he or she may be tormented by unfulfilled dreams, wondering, "Why did it happen? What did I do wrong? Why did I ignore my intuition?" With all of these "internal conversations" taking place at once, try to remember that the person you are trying to comfort probably can't hear a lot of what you are saying. You might have all sorts of advice to offer—ranging from why it happened to what the person can do in the future. But this is a time, for now, for you to practice conscious listening. Even though it might not sound like you are helping much at first, try rephrasing and reflecting—playing back what your friend seems to be feeling, what you see, or what you hear in your friend's voice. Playing back what you hear a friend saying can help release what is all locked up inside.* Until your friend can feel it—and stop trying to not feel it—only then will he or she be able to heal it, move on, and perhaps later benefit from your perspective.

*There are many professionals, from social workers to clergy to relationship counselors, who can help people navigate the lingering effects of a breakup. There are also a lot of excellent books (see Resources) that you can give your friend or read through first to see if there's a chapter or an exercise in the book that might be especially helpful.

Tuning Out of Your Head, Tuning In to Your Heart

Just as a horse can smell fear, people can feel energy around them. At one time or another, you have probably said, "I have a good feeling about this person; he (or she) gives off good vibes." You don't even know why you feel that way; it's just something you sense. The same goes for being in a conversation: the energy you bring to a healing conversation can be picked up by the person you are trying to support or comfort.

It's important to remember that we can affect other people's ability to heal by the energy we give off when we are with them. Your energy may be distracted (and thus cause you to tune others out) by being preoccupied with feeling that you don't know how to help. Or maybe you do know how to help but aren't sure how to offer your help or have it be accepted. All of this internal talk can tangle up the very healing presence you would like to be. When someone is talking to you about a painful or upsetting situation, don't you often find that your mind starts talking back? We think to ourselves, "I can't believe she . . . ," "I can't imagine . . . ," "I would never have done . . . ," "How awful," "I have no clue of what to do to help," or "I could never ask him that!" These are our internal conversations, and they are often understandably colored by an energy of our own judgment of what needs to be done, our agreement or disagreement with what someone is saying, our fear about what's happening to the other person, or our own worry about what to say or how to be. It's hard to stop the internal conversations from interfering with our ability and desire to listen.

One way to shift your energy and become an invitation for others to tune in to you on a more healing frequency is to get in touch with your own unexpressed anger, sadness, fear, judgment, or confusion. You may also want to appreciate that others whose help you're counting on may have their own fears about letting you down or may be reluctant to help because they don't know whether they can respond appropriately to your emotions. You may need to pause to acknowledge—to yourself or to others—how you are feeling. Taking a few minutes to do this may make it more comfortable for others to talk about their feelings or uncertainties, too.

So what do you do to acknowledge that you are running your own private sidebar conversation? And how do you get back into a healing connection with the person you are talking to? You could say something like this: "Allen, while you were talking to me about your father getting sicker and how it's so hard for you to know what to do, I've realized that I'm sitting here listening to you but thinking to myself about losing my own dad. I just wanted to tell you that I'm unexpectedly dealing with some of my own fears about how I would handle it if it happened to me."

When we don't let others know what's going on inside our head or our body, we can subtly make the people we are trying to support feel that we are bored, upset, judging them, or somehow disconnected. When you have the courage to be vulnerable enough to let others know what is coming up for you—either in your internal talk or in your feelings—it clears out the static that interferes with a healing frequency. This is one way you can create a caring presence by consciously tuning in your channels for listening. These are the moments that allow people to have a treasured "heart-to-heart" experience because no one is pretending.

- What do I have to do for myself in an awkward or unfamiliar situation to be able to listen in a way that is most helpful to the person I'm trying to comfort?

- How can I hold off asking questions for a while until I understand how the other person is feeling and how I'm feeling and appreciate what the other person might really need from me at this moment?

- What would it take for me to slow down my desire to make this person feel better right away?

- If I'm not giving this person advice or fixing the problem, how will I know that I am doing something helpful? What might some clues be that I could look for to let me know that "just listening" is enough?

- If I'm the one asking for help, and I'm not used depending on others, what could be a small step for me to take me in that direction the next time I need someone to lean on?

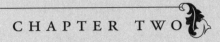

CHAPTER TWO

Health Matters

Test Results

🐎 *Getting the news or waiting to hear*

ONE DAY, YOU OR SOMEONE CLOSE TO YOU MAY GET A CALL FROM THE DOC-tor about distressing test results. As Jen discovered one night, this is a time when you want to turn to your doctor, family, and friends for the right words.

🐎 "You have an abnormal reading," the doctor told me and then rushed on to talk in terminology I didn't understand. Then the doc-tor mentioned something about my test result numbers being between two and four.

"What's normal?" I asked the doctor.

"One," she said, pausing for a few minutes before telling me the bad news that some of the cells were a four. "You need to see a spe-cialist, who will do a biopsy," she explained, rattling off facts I could tell she had told to many other women who'd had similar results.

By now I wanted to be treated like a person, not just a test result number. The thought flashed briefly through my mind, Maybe this isn't easy for the doctor either. Mostly, though, I just want the doctor to make it all be OK. I wanted to believe that it was a mistake. Then again, I couldn't help wondering whether I was to blame for bringing this upon myself. The conversation took only a few minutes, but I felt like it was taking forever to get the doctor to tell me what was really going on.

"Are we talking cancer?" I asked.

"Well, yes," the doctor said, as if it should have been clear to me by now. She went on to say, "The tests would be for cancer. We'll do a biopsy." This was supposed to reassure me. It didn't. It felt mechanical. We talked about insurance and which doctors I'd go to for follow-up tests. Now the conversation was about the business of medicine and procedures for working my way through the system.

"What's the best that could happen and what's the worst?" I asked the doctor.

"The best is that they take a scraping, it's not cancerous, and they kill off the cells by freezing them. The worst is, well, major surgery."

After hanging up, I felt like a statistic, like millions of women and men who get news like this and have to sit it out until they can reach some doctor's office, where they don't know anyone and are just another appointment referred to them for an abnormal test result. We're all waiting for an appointment. Waiting for more test results. Wondering, What if? and How did this happen? Asking, What next? I began thinking about what's really important in my life. I wondered how much time I had left—thinking to myself, Not many of us walk around thinking that this day or this week or this month could be our last. Not until we're facing the outcome of abnormal test results.

I wondered if I should call anyone. After all, maybe there is nothing to worry about. I don't want people feeling sorry for me either. What if nothing was really wrong and I'd sent a false alarm? I decided to talk to my sister. It turned out that she wasn't home but her husband tried to reassure me by saying matter-of-factly, "Look, tests can be wrong, so you'll go get another test."

I still needed to talk about all the thoughts zinging around in my head, so I called some close friends who are like parents to me. They took a down-to-earth approach to comforting me. First of all, they did not try to hide their dismay or their concern, "This is serious," they said. "Tell us more." Second, they didn't try to give me false assurances by saying, "Oh, honey, everything will be fine." (At this point, I'd like to think I'll be fine, but since no one really knows for sure, I don't want anyone insisting that I'll be fine because it makes me feel that I'm being silly to feel scared.) Third, they did make sure that I had confidence in my doctor; if I didn't, they were prepared to help me find another one. Fourth, they told me that it is normal to be scared.

Then my friends told me that it sounded as if I was saying that this was probably the biggest unknown I'd ever had to face. They were right. What was really bothering me wasn't that I didn't think I couldn't handle whatever might happen—it was not knowing that was so hard to take. They helped me realize this when they told me point blank, "It *is* a big deal, waiting to hear whether you have cancer, and we and others will help you through it, no matter what happens."

In the days that followed, while I waited for more tests, it was hard to shut off the voices that kept asking, "What if?" Little voices saying, "It's time." In literally minutes, everything had changed. I thought to myself, It *is* time—to live. One thing that helped me through the waiting was to remember my friends' phrase "no matter what happens." To me that phrase meant that whether it turned out to be a false alarm or the worst case, my friends wouldn't second-guess me or make me feel foolish. They'd just "be there" for me. As simple as that sounds, it meant a lot because it would be weeks before I'd learn how serious the problem was.

Those of us who've been through the experience of waiting for test results have another insight to offer friends and family: even if the tests show that nothing is medically wrong, the person you are trying to comfort may never feel the same. We have had a brush with the possibility of an altered or short-ened life. Even if everything is fine medically, we may feel a temporary or long-term heightened sense of our mortality. We have been inducted against our will into a fraternity or sorority where everyone has one thing in common: they have gone through waiting to get news that could change their life for-ever. They have lived briefly in a state of suspended animation, holding their breath, hoping for the best and afraid of the rest. They may need to talk about wanting to change their life—their job, their attitude, their habits, their pri-orities, or the way they treat others. It's not an overreaction. It's actually a way to cope with the what-ifs they've contemplated while waiting days or weeks to get their latest test results.

If you are the doctor or nurse delivering the news over the telephone, con-sider taking a few minutes to find out whether your patient is alone. You could ask if there is someone the patient can talk to after you finish your conversa-tion. As a patient, it's very hard to suddenly be thrust into a world of num-bers and medical probabilities that you'll have to take up with a stranger—the specialist you'll be sent to for more tests. Let your patients know what role your office will play to help get the care they may need if more tests bear bad news.

Several doctors told me that when they make calls bearing bad news, they are relieved when someone "only" has an abnormal test result. One admitted, "We sometimes forget that the fact that the results aren't conclusively life-threatening doesn't mean that the patient's world isn't turned upside down." A doctor or nurse can be the first to help a patient locate an anchor, no matter what happens.

If you are a spouse or significant other of someone awaiting test results, you also face difficult challenges. Consider this woman's experience while waiting to hear whether her melanoma had returned: "I felt such a sense of care when Joe finally put his arms around me and told me how scared he was of losing me. I had asked him two or three times before what he was feeling; I had the sense that I was the only one who was afraid! He didn't say much then, and when I asked him more about it, he explained that he was afraid that if he talked about his fear, he would be giving more power to the possibility that I might have cancer. I *do* understand what he was thinking, but I just wanted to feel empathy and care wrapped around me . . . and I am learning to ask for it."

Peaceful Warrior

When you want to help deal with a diagnosis

ONE NIGHT, A GROUP OF FRIENDS GOT AN E-MAIL MESSAGE FROM ELISA-
beth after she had learned that her husband's supposedly benign tumor was
cancerous and required immediate surgery and chemotherapy. She wrote, "I
am looking for advice from any of you who have faced cancer. What kind of
support was valuable to you from a spouse or loved one? This is so overwhelming to me, and I still cannot believe this has happened." What do you
do when you first learn that someone you know has been diagnosed with a
serious illness and his or her loved one is asking for help?

There are times when people in trouble don't want to hear your story
about how you got through a tough time. They need to talk first about their
own feelings and concerns. In this case, however, Elisabeth was specifically asking friends for any insights they could share to help her and her husband, Ron,
cope. I wrote her the following note (which has been edited for publication):

❧ Elisabeth:

When a friend of mine was suddenly diagnosed with cancer, my sister, who at the time was an oncology nurse, taught me something valuable. In her years of caring for cancer patients, she'd learned that when you are diagnosed with cancer, suddenly you feel like your life is out of control. The worst thing people can do is to take over the patient's life. She encourages us to try to give patients some emotional space to make decisions about their life, their care, and their treatment. It's hard for us to resist taking over for our relatives, siblings, or friends. It's hard to *be with* the agony of their not knowing what to do. But helping them get information leads them to making better decisions about what is best for them.

Ron may have read Dan Millman's book, *Way of the Peaceful Warrior.* If he hasn't, I suggest he consider it. It offers lessons in how to fight *for* your health, not against an illness or injury. The book presents a simple story about how our attitude can help us heal. Maybe what I am trying to say is that in the onrush of the overwhelming issues of living—diagnosis with a disease, dealing with doctors, having our routines upset—sometimes it is the words and stories of others that break through the clutter.

While I can't know how all this will turn out for you and Ron, I encourage you to read and share and journal and yell and be quiet together. When you feel angry, if you do, let that be OK, too. Spouses who have dealt with cancer have needed someone that they could turn to and say, "What about me?" It's not being selfish. It's being human.

A few weeks later, Ron sent a note to all of us. Reading it says a lot about how to support friends during an illness and about how to communicate frankly with them if you are the one who is ill.

    🪶 Dear Folks,

I hope you will forgive me for communicating in a newsletter rather than individually as I prefer, but it's the easiest way for me right now. I've always played my cards rather close to my vest where any aches, pains, or illnesses I've had were concerned, so "publicity" like this is a little uncomfortable for me. However, talking to my friends about what's going on with me is helpful, so that's why I'm doing it.

I've been reading a lot about cancer, chemotherapy, and life-threatening diseases, and there are several nonmedical things that you can do for yourself that are very therapeutic. Expressing your feelings about what is happening to you is one of those things. Hearing from your friends and family, laughing a lot, and doing things you enjoy are also highly curative.

Some of you have confessed to me that it is difficult for you to talk about these things with me. There are various reasons for this, all of which I understand. I just want you to know that it doesn't bother me to say "cancer," that death is not something I fear (I guess not living—as in quality of life—is a worse fear), and I am optimistic about the future, whatever amount of time that happens to be. So if you're comfortable with where I am with this and want to talk about it with me, I'll be fine.

All these things help give me peace of mind. I owe every one of you for aiding me in this process. The golf you've mercifully watched me try to play after my abdominal surgery; the jokes you've told me on e-mail, in your cards, at the poker game, and on the phone; the visits; the breakfasts and lunches you've asked me to have with you; and your prayers and thoughts have helped immensely. They have lifted my spirits, and I am grateful to all of you for that.

At this moment, I'm really happy. I realize that I will have some down times as I go through my treatment and go about my daily business, but my hope is that those will be minimal. With people like you in my life, I know that will be the case.

Some people believe it is therapeutic to share your feelings about fighting an illness. Ron is one of those people. However, your friends or family members may still play their cards close to the vest the way Ron did before he was ill. Not everyone is as open as Ron was in letting friends know that it's fine to talk about dying. He also told them that it was fine if they didn't want to talk about it.

If you aren't sure how a person you are trying to comfort wants to be supported, one way you can show that you care is to become educated about his or her disease:

- Go to the library or get on the Internet to learn as much as you can.
- Call organizations like the American Cancer Society and other groups with information about the disease your friend or relative has.
- Call your own doctor's office to find out where you can get more information about this disease.

You don't have to become an expert on the disease or condition, but you can at least share in some of what your friend is learning. You *can* learn about research, treatments and their possible side effects, alternative approaches, and recovery. You can learn the vocabulary about the disease and understand what is good news and what might be bad news so that you don't find yourself offering either false hopes or jumping to premature conclusions. Knowing that you made the effort to become informed will show how much you care.

Facing Surgery

Before, during, and after

Some of us have seen so many television shows about surgery that it can seem pretty routine. However, that's not the case when it's happening to you. Friends have taught me that there are a lot of ways we can support one another before, during, and after surgery.

"I wish someone could give me the headline recommendation of what works," a friend said one night shortly before major surgery. He felt swamped by well-meaning friends who were flooding him with articles, names of people to call for information, books, and the like. "I know they are trying to be helpful," he acknowledged, "but right now I feel like I have three full-time jobs—running a company, getting it ready for me to be gone for a while, and running down information to make decisions about my health."

Whether you are facing major or minor surgery, it can be overwhelming to realize just how much you don't know and how much help you may need while you are recovering. It's as if you must prepare for "before," "during," and "after" the event long before it happens. It helps to offer people facing surgery just one concrete, digestible piece of counsel or information that focuses on a concern or need they have. Examples include how to find the right doctor, alternative healers, selecting a hospital, information about options they may have, home help, financial support, and how to talk to family and colleagues about the pending surgery, recovery, and any special help the patients will need.

You could also offer to do something specific for them (take them to and from the hospital, mow the lawn, water the plants, pick up the kids, clean the house, and so on) rather than ask them, "What can I do to help?" Often people don't know—nor can they anticipate—what they'll need. They will appreciate it if you suggest something simple that you could do. Your offer to help could sound something like "I can arrange my schedule to take you to surgery and to pick you up. It's something I'd need someone to do for me if I were having surgery. I'd certainly be glad to do this for you."

I'll never forget what my friend JoAnn did for me when I underwent laser surgery for the removal of precancerous cells. She offered to pray for me. (It's not something I would think to ask anyone to do for me.) She didn't just pray for me; she prayed for the doctor, the nurse, and the equipment. Yes, the equipment. On the day of the surgery, I told the doctor and his nurse that my friend was praying for all of us and for the equipment. The doctor looked up and smiled. "Your friend has the right idea," he said. "This is the first time we've used this new equipment in this office, and the nurse who is helping out doesn't usually assist in these procedures. And it *is* Friday the thirteenth!"

Sometimes we try to make our friends feel better by instantly telling them, "You'll be fine" or "You can handle this, after all you've been through." Though these comments may sound reassuring, when people are first dealing with facing surgery, they need to be able to be scared or mad or anxious. They don't want everyone telling them, "You will be fine." They may want to yell back, "Yeah, how do *you* know?" Or maybe they don't want to get their hopes up too high. While they do want the surgery to be successful, they also need someone they can talk to about any concerns they have about its being unsuccessful. If most of the people around them are, in effect, shutting off that kind of talk because they want to believe that everything will be fine, then the patients' fears have nowhere to go but around and around in their head. It can help if we gently ask, "Is there anything you are concerned about that you'd like to talk through with me?" Or we can say something like "It must be difficult not knowing exactly how things will turn out." Then pause and let a soft silence create an opportunity for them to reflect.

It's normal for many people who are facing surgery to be concerned about dealing with anesthesia, postoperative pain, possible side effects of prescription pain killers, and recovery regimens. You can help by either tracking down the information they need or brainstorming ways for them to get it themselves. I remember feeling a bit frantic about the kind of anesthesia that would be used on me when I went in for "minor" foot surgery. I had a choice of three hospitals where the surgery could be performed. My sister, a nurse anesthetist, strongly encouraged me to call the anesthesia department of each hospital and then choose which hospital to go to based on how the anesthesiologist responded to my questions. It would never have occurred to me that I could call the anesthesiologist, but my sister explained that the less nervous a patient is, the easier the surgery is for both the patient and the surgical team.

In the end, I chose one particular hospital because the anesthesiologist patiently explained the process. Even more important, he acknowledged how I was feeling. "You know, Nance," he said, "when surgery is happening to someone else, it's called minor; when it's happening to you, it's major." I felt

I could relax a bit about being operated on at a place where, instead of trying to convince me that I had nothing to worry about, the anesthesiologist understood that I was worried. Our conversation lasted five minutes, but it enabled me to go into the operating room less anxious about the surgery. I know it was a little thing to him. To me it was everything.

Several friends have discovered a way to ask for support on the day of surgery. You tell your well-wishers what time your surgery is scheduled. Then ask them to pause at the time of your surgery to send you positive energy, imagine everything happening smoothly in the operating room, and imagine the tissue beginning to heal. The idea comes from a very practical book, *Prepare for Surgery: Heal Faster,* written by Peggy Huddleston. She suggests that you ask friends to "wrap you in a pink blanket of healing energy thoughts." Several doctors have found that using this "healing blanket of energy" approach is so calming that they require their patients to read the book. One friend went into the operating room with her pink blanket wrapped around her feet. When the surgical staff tried to remove it, the doctor said, "Please leave it. She's wrapped up in a lot of good wishes, and we can use all the healing energy she can get!"

Sometimes we can feel like the day of surgery is, as one friend first put it, "D-Day." But on the day before that friend's operation, we decided to call it "R-Day," the day that certain parts of her body that she no longer needed would be "released."

Just How Do You Ask for Help?

Making your own wish list

JUST HOW *DO* YOU TELL PEOPLE THAT YOU NEED THEIR HELP?

One of the most wonderful examples of asking for help arrived in the mail one day from a woman who founded an unusual nonprofit group—a troupe of specially trained clowns! Jeannie trains, schedules, and supports a year-round volunteer program that brings clowns to visit children in area hospitals. When she learned that she had cancer, she needed to let her clowns (and friends) know that some things would change and some things wouldn't. She wrote us all a letter in which she made specific requests about what would, and wouldn't, be most helpful to her at this time.

> Dear Clowns:
>
> This letter is not easy for me to write. December 7, the day before my birthday (you all sent great greetings), I was told I have breast

cancer. I had surgery December 1 to remove some atypical cells. In the biopsy they incidentally found some malignant cells. How lucky that was! I know you must be thinking—Jeannie is crazy, but these cells, I was told, would *not* have shown up on a mammogram! The doctor who gave me the news said, "If we'd found this in a year, it might not have been so good."

I feel blessed and incredibly lucky that they did find it. I want to let you *all* know that I will be *fine!* This whole process started in September, and in the last three months, I feel like I have been on a "rolly coaster."

Forgive me for sending you all this letter. I had originally wanted to personally phone each of you, but a woman I met said, "Oh, no, you can't make 35 phone calls. You need to conserve your energy. Write a letter." And that sounded right.

Last summer I read a book on nonprofits that said something like, "The sign of a successful leader is that if he/she leaves, the organization can run without him/her." I *know* that if I take a clown "sabbatiful," the troupe can easily go on without me. I am *not* leaving but do need to take some time off to heal and deal with all of the decisions that must be made.

I know I must delegate too! I need time to gather info in terms of treatment, use creative visualization, write in my journal, rest, and heal. Some of you may be wondering: What can I do to help?

- Office help—e-mail if you can help anytime with office stuff.
- Recommendations of great movies, music, and wonderful inspirational quotes you have—I *love* great quotes!
- Your good thoughts, prayers, white light, and love.

- Your calls would mean a lot to me, but unless you need me to call you back, I probably won't. I would love to hear your voice but have been told by many friends that I'll need to conserve my energy and not be on the phone a lot.

I love you sweet clowns!

Jeannie

Jeannie did friends and family a favor by letting us know what she needed *and* what she *didn't* need. She made specific requests we could honor. Writing us, in advance of her surgery, saved her from endless calls asking, "What can I do?" *She took responsibility for asking for what she wanted,* rather than waiting until she was swamped with calls or visitors. She helped us understand that healing would be her full-time job for a while and that she needed to focus her energy on getting well, not on responding to well-wishers. She even guided us in the kinds of thoughts we could have of her—in essence encouraging us to "send me your prayers and love, not your fears."

Paciencia
Recovering from depression

HAVE YOU EVER HAD A FRIEND OR RELATIVE WHO SEEMED DEPRESSED AND you weren't sure how serious it was or what to do? Helping people get through depression requires patience—on your part and on theirs. Sometimes it's best for them to talk to a professional, especially if they are having trouble getting out of bed, going to work, taking care of their family, or functioning on an everyday level. That's a more serious form of clinical depression where your support may come in the form of helping them get expert guidance.

Sometimes, though, especially in the beginning, people who are feeling down need a good listener. Occasionally, sharing a story of your own can give them a new look at their problem. These lessons were given to me one day when I was feeling like I would never walk again. It had been two months since foot surgery. After months of pain and treatment, my foot wasn't heal-ing; in fact, it was getting worse.

As the unwelcome sluggish feeling of being hopelessly and unexpectedly depressed set in, my massage therapist asked me if I was open to hearing a story about how he had learned to get through his bouts of depression, triggered by an injury that was slow to heal. I appreciated that he paused to see whether I needed to keep telling him how I felt or was ready for a fresh perspective. His checking in with me to let me decide what I needed made it easier for me to hear Bill's story:

> ❧ Let me tell you about my grandmother. She was only thirteen when she came to this country from Portugal. She didn't speak English. She didn't have a job. She left her family behind. She came to Massachusetts to start a new life. It wasn't easy. She learned how to speak English by working as a housekeeper for a local New Bedford family. She learned how to endure many things.
>
> When I was growing up, she was the person everyone would call for advice and for perspective. When everything looked dark and gloomy, the one you would call would be my grandmother. What she offered people was more than just her words; it was her way of being in the world. In Portuguese we refer to someone like my grandmother as someone who has *paciencia,* patience.
>
> First she would listen to the caller. In fact, she was so good at listening that the telephone operators, the old-fashioned kind, would get on the phone and tell everyone to hang up because my grandmother's callers were tying up the party lines we shared with neighbors. She would encourage people to have faith that things will work out. Then she would say, "You must have patience."
>
> When I was injured and doctor after doctor couldn't figure out what was wrong with me, much less heal me, I began to lose hope. I

kept thinking that the next person I would see for help would be the one to put it all together. The pain shot up and down my leg and my back; at times it was unbearable. What was worse was not knowing when, or if, it would ever go away.

Bill realized that to get better, he would need more than just a doctor who could fix his leg. "I needed someone who could help me deal with an overwhelming sense of depression," he explained. "I knew it was time to talk to a therapist, which I did. One day, my therapist introduced me to a little book that put it all together for me," he continued, "and helped me understand that the only way I was going to get through my depression was, well, to get through it. To endure. Not endure like tough it out or be numb to it. But endure the way my grandmother did. To have *paciencia.* To have faith that even though I couldn't quite see how things were going to work out, if I could endure, somehow things would get better. The trick was to not give up hope even when I didn't have anyone or anything to pin my hopes on."

After dealing with his own dark times, Bill said, "I realized just how important my grandmother had been to her friends and family. She was a healer who helped people by reminding them to have faith in themselves and in things that they couldn't yet see. *"Paciencia,"* she would say, *"paciencia."*

Then Bill gave me a copy of the book that had helped him so much during his dark days. It is called *How to Heal Depression* by Harold Bloomfield and Peter McWilliams, the coauthors of the popular and helpful book *How to Survive the Loss of a Love* (Melba Colgrove, Harold Bloomfield, and Peter McWilliams). The way Bill offered me the book was very sensitive. He didn't give it to me as if it would solve my problem or give me all the answers. He offered it as a way to help me get perspective. Giving a book to help people begin to understand their pain is one way you can support friends who are baffled by a difficult circumstance.

Depression can take lots of forms. It can be big or small. It can sneak up on you or overwhelm you. It can show up for no apparent reason or appear like clockwork when you hit a rough spot. It's not just a matter of attitude or willpower, either. It's all wrapped up in the way our brains receive and process life. Understandably, many of us try to cheer up people who are depressed. That's rarely what they need. They need us to understand that they're feeling as if they live in a room without doors or windows, a room with no way out. Before we try to convince them that there *is* a way out of the darkness, remember the power of reflection. Take a few moments to calmly understand how walled in they feel. They need you to have patience with their impatience, too.

About the same time I was learning this lesson about *paciencia* and depression, an old friend and I unexpectedly wound up talking about her wish for her husband to see a psychiatrist. She felt he needed an expert to help him with problems she couldn't deal with on her own. Three weeks earlier, I'd been with a group of executives who had tried to tell one of their colleagues that his problems needed a professional; his issues were beyond the group's scope of expertise.

Both my friend and the executives had said to someone they care about, "Look, I can't help you; you need to see a therapist." I suggest that before you say that to others, pause and put yourself in their shoes. When someone tells you, "Look, you need help and I can't give you what you need," it's a wake-up call. It can hurt or shock you or even confirm what you've known all along and didn't want to accept. The trouble is, the person who needs help may not be in shape to go out and find the right therapist. Or as my friend said of her husband, "He's afraid that if he starts down that road with a therapist, it will never end." Anything you can do to compassionately acknowledge your friends' or loved ones' concerns about therapy and help them confidentially get the referral they need will enable them to take an important step toward healing.

Trying to help someone find a therapist can be easier said than done. If you don't know one personally, you could begin by asking friends for recommendations. You can call your family physician for guidance or call your local community mental health center to learn how they recommend you help someone who may need a therapist for the first time in their life.

Is the Doctor In?

🐟 *Making the most of your time as a patient or as a doctor*

Most of us go to a doctor because something is wrong and we want to feel better. Sometimes it's just for a checkup; other times it's for a serious problem. Often, however, healing takes place not because of a drug, a procedure, or an operation. Healing can begin in the space of a few carefully chosen words that are exchanged when the doctor *or* the patient takes the time to connect as human beings.

"Whew, it's cold in here," Dr. DiSciullo murmured, smiling sheepishly at his first office patient of the morning. "Let me turn the heat up," he said, squeezing himself between the examining table and the heating unit along the floor as he reached awkwardly to turn up the thermostat. "Sorry about that. I'll be right back after I take a quick call."

Minutes later, when the doctor returned, he talked to his patient about whether she had any complaints. She didn't—not about what he was checking for, to see if the precancerous lesions in her cervix had turned into anything serious. "No complaints in your department," she said, wondering whether she should mention to him the ten-pound weight gain, the loss of energy, the not being sure how to handle early middle age. After all, he was her gynecologist, not her internist or a therapist. But she figured, Hey, he seems to care about my being cold; why not talk to him about my concerns? So she asked him whether maybe an old thyroid problem had kicked up and contributed to the weight gain, the depression, the lethargy, or whether that was nonsense.

The doctor did his exam and found nothing of immediate concern. A few minutes later, they were back in his office next to the examining room. He gently asked his patient how she felt about her life. "Are things any better?" She told him she seemed to have adjusted to all the accidents, injuries, and changes going on in her body. She never knew what to expect next. He smiled and thanked her when she asked how his wife was recovering from her sudden lumpectomy—an emergency where he'd found himself on the other side of the doctor's desk, as the husband of a patient.

Dr. DiSciullo began talking about what it takes to help doctors find the time or make the effort to listen to their patients in this world of "managed care." His patient knew that the doctor was on a well-run schedule this morning and that he rarely kept patients waiting. She wanted to respect his scheduling process, which she certainly appreciated. She knew he had to bring their time together to an end, and yet she also knew he wanted to make sure he had heard everything she needed to share. Suddenly, he started explaining to her the special steps he and his staff take to make sure his patients feel that they come first.

"We had to make an extra effort in this building when we renovated other offices to make sure that there were no sinks in the room," said Dr. DiSciullo. "When you turn to wash your hands, you turn your back to the patient. We didn't want that. We figured we should go to another room to take care of that. The examining room is for the patient, strictly for the patient. We also made sure that none of our examining rooms have phones. We are there for that patient. If a doctor needs to take a call, he or she asks to be excused, leaves the room briefly, and returns to give full attention to the patient again. It's getting harder to keep this policy of ours—all the new offices they build these days come with phones and sinks. They just don't get how important it is to take the time to listen, even if it's only five minutes.

"We used to have a P.A. [physician's assistant] who had that gift," Dr. DiSciullo reminisced. "She had a way with patients. They used to tell me that they couldn't believe she only had spent a few minutes with them because it felt much longer. I once watched her do her intake process—four minutes, but in that four minutes she gave the patient her complete attention. Even to me it felt that they had been talking for much longer. I wish we could teach more people in our profession to take whatever time they have with a patient and make the most of it."

If you are a doctor and can focus on one patient, for even a few minutes— undistracted by thoughts of other patients or pending calls—it will feel as if you have been with them for an even longer time. It's called being present for that patient in the time you have.

It had been over a year since Dr. DiSciullo's patient had seen him. He didn't know it, but she'd come close to canceling the appointment because of a nasty winter storm. But secretly she didn't want to come and confront getting older, nearing menopause, being examined for cells she couldn't see that could possibly change her life. She wasn't sure she would have mentioned anything important to her doctor if he hadn't listened with something more than a stethoscope. Something more than his ears told him what to tune in to that morning. How did she feel at the end of the visit? Just a little more human. That's what can happen when the doctor is truly *in*.

What's the Difference Between a Cure and Healing?

Living with chronic pain

What do you say to someone who has a pain or condition that doesn't go away? Many people live with arthritis, a bad back, chronic fatigue, multiple sclerosis, fibromyalgia, and other conditions for which there may be treatments but there doesn't seem to be a cure. It can be hard to know how to greet, let alone spend time with, someone who's always living with an undercurrent of discomfort. Do you even raise the subject or ignore it?

One day, I realized that there is a difference between hoping for a cure and finding a way to live the life we've been given, even if it means living with chronic pain. I'm not sharing these reflections about my life because my life is a daily tragedy. It's not. I'm sharing these thoughts as an example of how you can have a healing conversation with yourself. You may also discover a new appreciation for the obstacles and the pathways to healing—for yourself or for someone you know who is living with a chronic condition.

Do you ever have days when you don't know whether to give up or give in? That's the story of my life these past few years. I haven't known whether to quit or to surrender. I think I've been dancing at the edge of resignation and surrender for a long time. Maybe you know someone who has been in that dance, too. Resignation as in "I give up." Surrender as in "OK, I accept my fate and give in to what life is giving me."

The trouble I've been having is all tied up around learning how to live with chronic pain. For a long time, I think I didn't even know that I was in pain. I toughed my way through emotional disappointments by being strong. By taking charge. By doing my best to make someone else's life better. The trouble with this kind of thinking is that I wasn't really living my life. I was living *around* it, through other people.

It's not that I haven't acknowledged my problems to friends, family, clients, healers, and myself. It's just that I've been looking for a cure. I've been looking to be pain-free. I think I've set my sights on climbing the wrong mountain. I have a question that I pose to clients that instantly helps them focus on the matter at hand. Here's the question: When our time together is over, what does success look like?

What did success look like for me? The absence of pain. But something happened this week when I came down with a strange laryngitis or flu. My body has literally been falling apart for years due a condition in which the ligaments no longer hold the joints in place, so they collapse and dislocate and the tissues tighten up to hold the joints together. However, I rarely get sick. But this week, knocked down by a persistent flu that turned my back into cement and my body to lead, I suddenly decided I'd been going about this healing thing all wrong: for years, I'd been making healing a fight, a quest, if you will, against my body. I'd been trying to break down the knots and the stiffness with massage, electric current, acupuncture, anti-inflammatories, heat packs, ice packs, chiropractic adjustments, orthotics, shots, surgery, and physical therapy.

In conversations with myself, I'd wondered, Why was I born with ankles that collapsed instead of holding my little kid body up? Was I born weak to learn how to ask for help? Was I born weak to learn how to get strong? Was I born with a body that breaks down so that I could understand that often it takes a breakdown to generate a breakthrough?

It seems that my "job" early in life was to ignore the pain and dance my way to strength, literally. The doctor sent me to dancing school at age three to try to strengthen my ankles. Then riding at age six, taking four-foot jumps on a sixteen-hands horse named Major. Water skiing at seven. Gymnastics in high school. Hiking and rock climbing at eighteen. I took to the physical challenges, unaware of the limitations of a body that was apparently (I learned later in life) born to fall apart; the ligaments were so stretchy that they wouldn't hold the joints in place. I'd just strap on the Ace bandages, slug down the Advil, put my torn cartilage and ligaments "on ice," and march on. What was my body trying to tell me?

What looked like a strength—born flexible—would become a limitation when my overly flexible body couldn't be counted on, in middle age, to hold it all together. That's when I *got it*. I'd been born trying to hold it all together my whole life. That's why my body is falling apart—to help me realize that life isn't about holding it all together. Life is about disappointments, limits, things that don't work out, imperfect knees, ankles, backs, and joints. Life isn't about being so flexible that, unmindful of our own needs, we can be all things to all people. Life is about letting ourselves (and others) in—not about toughing it out on our own.

So at the doorstep of so-called middle-age, I've decided to embark on a research project. Here is the inquiry I'm pursuing: What *is* healing?

I think a lot of us have *healing* confused with *being cured*.

What if healing has to do with coming to terms with life? What if it's about accepting who you were born to be or not to be? What if it's about forgiving yourself for the limits you were born with or developed later in life? What if healing is to forgive others who may have contributed to those limits?*

Maybe healing is also about never understanding why certain aches and pains are in our life and learning from them anyway. It's about realizing that yes, other people have far worse pain than we do, and our pain isn't really our pain. It's a pain that is part of a continuum of life that connects us to other people who live with their aches and pains.

Many people, of all ages and faiths and no faith, live at the intersection of healing and hurt. They live at the edge of hope and hopelessness. That's why even though I thought I was an expert in this breakdown-to-breakthrough healing work, I've decided to start over again and ask the question: What *is* healing? With so many of us at the threshold of midlife and beyond, I feel that it's the right question for us to be asking. Maybe more of us can use pain as a compass to help navigate the river of life all around us.

---

*Author Carolyn Myss provides helpful insights into these questions in her book and tape series, *Why People Don't Heal . . . and How They Can.* I've found the tapes extremely helpful and have shared them with clients and friends.

Here are some guidelines to help you comfort someone with a chronic condition:

- Please don't make asking us about our health your first question. We are more than our condition. If we need to tell you how we're feeling, we'll let you know.

- If you've discovered new information about our condition, please don't be offended if we don't follow up right away or even take your suggestions. After trying many approaches, we may (temporarily) have run out of energy to try something else; we're tired of getting our hopes up. Days or months later, however, your information may be just what we need.

- Even if there are activities that we can no longer do with you, maybe there's a way we can still enjoy being with you: If we can't ski, we can read by the fire; if we can't paddle, we can ride along in a double kayak; if we can't dance, we can still enjoy the music!

- Please realize that although our condition may not improve, it helps if we can make as much out of our life as we can instead of focusing on what we can't do.

What About Me?

Supporting the caregiver

Most of the time, our attention and efforts to provide comfort are focused on the person who is ill. However, this story about how one couple dealt with a health crisis reminds us that there's a whole other side to the story.

When Wyllys was unexpectedly diagnosed with prostate cancer, he got a lot of attention. From his girlfriend, Marianne. From his kids. From his doctors and his friends. He had lots to think about. Which course of treatment? How to deal with his love life? What would the quality of his life be?

Some days Wyllys was sad, some days he was mad, and some days he was frantically trying to find out as much as he could. He was struggling with decisions, information overload, and having to be the one to eventually choose what to do.

Marianne spent hours with him, with the doctors, with the experts, and with the therapists learning how they could fight, and then live with, prostate cancer. They had to deal with questions about impotence, incontinence, love-making, self-esteem, postsurgical complications, and what might happen if the cancer returned after radioactive isotope treatment.

For hours, days, and weeks, Marianne laughed and cried with the man she loved. She was trying to be there for him in ways she had never imagined. Then one day, she wrote a friend a note saying that suddenly she realized that she was grieving as well. She felt she was losing something—a way of life they had enjoyed for three years. Suddenly everything had changed. While she felt it was important for her to be the loving, dutiful, stand-by-your-man friend and lover, all at once it hit her that she felt lonely. Who could she turn to and say, "What about me?"

Marianne needed a nonjudgmental place to worry about her future, her quality of life, and how long she could continue to be there for him. It didn't mean she loved him any less, but she didn't know how to share this with her friends or family without sounding selfish. After all, his very life was at risk; for her, it was her heart and her soul mate that were at risk.

It's important to pay attention to the needs of the spouse, family, and friends of a person who is going through a rough time. They need someone to ask how they are doing. Someone they can complain to, worry with, and not feel like they are being anything less than thoughtful and loving. Someone they can tell "I've never been so scared in my life" without that person trying to reassure them by saying, "Oh, you're strong; I know you can handle it." Finally, they need someone who won't judge them when they ask the simple question, "What about me?"

If someone you know is the caregiver for a loved one who is ill, think about sending the caregiver a "hang in there" card, sending a gift, offering to do household chores, or taking the caregiver out for a break. When you call, don't immediately ask how the patient is; first pause for a minute to acknowledge the effects that this situation is having on the caregiver.

You can also gently say something like, "I'm concerned about you, too. Are you getting the care that *you* need?" A caregiver who is feeling overwhelmed may appreciate your offer to brainstorm or research whether supplementary community or professional assistance is available. If it's appropriate and you feel capable enough or are willing to learn, you can offer to provide some respite care so that your friend can get out for a while—for a few hours, a day, or a weekend. Don't hesitate to also offer to do something as mundane as grocery shopping, picking up the kids, or running errands.

Caregivers will have days when they may want company so that they don't feel quite so alone. Or they may want you to help them do things that they used to do with their loved one but now can't manage to do on their own. For example, Mary Kay discovered that trying to decorate the Christmas tree with her husband, now that he had Alzheimer's, was impossibly frustrating for them both. She'd thought about giving up completely until she told her friend Kelly about her experience. Kelly didn't live nearby but wanted to try to help. She thought for a few minutes and then asked Mary Kay, "Why don't you invite a bunch of people over to help you do it? They can engage your husband in a totally different activity if that's what it takes for him to not get frustrated but still be included."

"I never would have thought of this wonderful solution to a problem I thought I had to solve myself," Mary Kay explained. There are days when caregivers need your company, and there are days when caregivers need to get away—not to do errands or to see a movie or even to visit others but to just be alone with their thoughts. Your gift of respite time means all the more if they don't have to worry about what you think they should be doing with it.

Second Sight

When a disability becomes an ability

I'VE GOT SOME BAD NEWS TO TELL YOU," SANTINA SAID, GETTING STRAIGHT to the reason she'd called. "For no apparent reason, I'm losing the sight in my right eye—everything's blurry. The doctors have done tests, but so far they can't find a cause or a cure. This can't be happening to me; I won't accept it. My husband says I should stop going off the deep end over this and quit imagining the worst. The hard part is, I can't stop thinking about 'what if . . . ?' I guess I just shouldn't think about it."

At first I didn't know what to say. I didn't know whether I should say that I couldn't imagine what it was like to be going through this or whether I should just listen some more to find out what she needed. Santina and I talked for a while about the doctors she'd been to and about their prognosis. Then I asked her what she needed from me right now in our conversation. "I need to talk about the what-ifs," she said, "and I *don't* want to beat around the bush!"

"Let's go for it," I said. "What's the worst that could happen?" I asked her. "That you would be permanently blind?"

"Oh, no," she said, "I haven't even let myself think that far. I guess the worst that could happen is that I'd lose the sight in one eye."

"OK," I went on, "and what's the worst that could happen if that happened?"

"Well," she paused, "I guess I could still read and drive because I do have one good eye. It seems that I have two kinds of vision. Actually, come to think of it, I was experimenting the other day and holding my hand over my good eye to see what I could see with my blurry eye. You know what? I see things as if they have no edges."

"So let me see if I understand what's going on here," I said, rephrasing what I thought she'd said *and* meant. "You're afraid that you might lose your sight, and you sound nervous about what that could be like. You are able to see the world without edges, as if things look softer to you?"

"Yes, yes," she interrupted. "I was thinking, What if I could help other people see things as I saw them: soft and out of focus? Maybe they could see things with a fresh perspective, too. What would that be like?"

Santina and I had just taken the time to "reframe" her problem so that she could see it from a different view. As the saying goes, "Where a door closes, a window opens"—but sometimes people need help finding the window.

After listening to Santina for a while, it felt like the right time to ask if I could tell her a story about what I learned when, after a concussion years ago, I lost my sense of smell and sense of taste. She said she'd like to hear the story. I told her that many people said things like, "Oh, that must be awful." Or they'd ask, "Don't you miss chocolate?" They couldn't understand that there were unexpected advantages to "losing" these abilities. While I couldn't taste the flavors, suddenly I noticed texture and freshness. While I couldn't smell fragrances, I also enjoyed not smelling fumes, body odors, and skunks. Disorienting? Yes, even dangerous. Miss chocolate? You bet. Did I sharpen other senses? Absolutely, sometimes giving me an edge others didn't have. I lived in a sort of "lost and found." I also told her that every once in a while, after someone had again said, "It must be awful," I would gently let the person know that losing an ability isn't always a disability; it has its advantages, too.

Losing our sight isn't something any of us would choose. For my friend, it was especially devastating, or so she first thought. You see, Santina is an artist—a gifted watercolorist. After talking today, though, we decided that maybe what she had lost is her vision the way she used to know it, but maybe what she has found is second sight.

This message—of appreciating that when you lose an ability, you may gain another one—is beautifully shared in the movie *At First Sight*, based on a book written by Dr. Oliver Sacks. It's the true story of Shirl Jennings, who lost his sight at the age of three and had it briefly restored as the result of an experimental operation. The operation's effects were temporary, and soon he was blind again. However, he explained to a conference of medical professionals, there's more to seeing than sight—a concept to remember when someone we care for may be losing an ability we can't imagine living without: "As a blind man I think that I see better than I did while sighted. Because I don't really think we see with our eyes. We live in darkness when we don't look at what's real about ourselves, about others, and about life. No operation can do that. When you see what's real about yourself, then you see a lot and you don't need eyes for that." The film makes an important point:

people don't always want to be fixed. Sometimes they need to be accepted the way they are.*

When you find yourself in a conversation with someone who is upset or confused, you can try to gently rephrase what you have heard so far. Then you can pause and say something like "I can hear you are upset, and I want to be helpful to you right now, but I'm not sure what you need from me." Take a breath or two before you go on to explain, "It would help me to know how you'd like me to listen. Do you think you need to vent? Do you want resources? Do you want advice, or do you want to just talk?" Remember to make sure that the energy behind your words isn't abrupt or doesn't seem as if you are trying to figure things out. You want the other person to understand that you are pausing to connect on the most supportive wavelength.

*At First Sight is a feature film based on "To See or Not See," a clinical portrait in An Anthropologist on Mars by Dr. Oliver Sacks (Random House, 1995). At First Sight screenplay by Steve Leavitt and Rob Cowan. Produced by Rob Cowen. Directed and produced by Irwin Winkler. Released by MGM, January 1999.

When the Bough Breaks

When you can't see their pain

It's only a broken arm," Roberta said, "but everything's changed."

She'd slipped at home putting on her stockings. Gave herself a solid break. Sitting there perched on the ottoman at the Valentine's Day party talking to someone she'd never met before, she looked tired. Cheerful, but tired. As if she could barely hold up the cast-wrapped arm held tightly to her chest with a heavy leather sling. Managing to eat, now, with her left hand. Not making a big deal about what was really no big deal. "It's just a broken arm, after all, not a broken heart," she explained.

What was causing Roberta's pain wasn't just her broken arm, but how would we know that at first glance? Regardless of whether we know people well or are meeting them for the first time, we rarely know what's going on underneath the surface after they've had an accident. The wake of an accident is often a time for tuning our own energy down into a lower gear so that we can absorb what others want to unravel to a listener who has no personal agenda.

It turns out that Roberta mends broken hearts and broken lives for a living. Really. It's what she's done, day in and day out, for years. People pay her to listen to their stories of loss and hope and sadness and fear and pain. Patients who have been holding back what hurts until they can't hold it back anymore. She's the one they call to talk to about their fears because she's their therapist.

There she sat on Valentine's Eve, politely talking to a stranger about her work. Then she looked up and confessed that she was feeling a bit out of sorts. No, it wasn't the sangria punch. It wasn't even the pain. It was actually the shock of the whole accident. The fact that she, who normally helped put other people back together, she, the healer, was feeling broken down. And it wasn't just the pain from the throbbing arm or the weariness. It was the shock of the whole accident that had, unbidden, released feelings she'd forgotten that she had. Feelings about living alone. About being hurt and being on her own. About being the one who has to take care of herself when she mostly takes care of others.

She was realizing that she'd been numb to a lot of regular everyday pain about the way she was living her life. Pain that she wouldn't normally allow to come through her unconsciously crafted fences. Until now. Until she couldn't hold it back anymore. Until she met a stranger who had nothing else on her mind but to listen with empathy.

"Funny," Roberta said, "I've never felt less put together, less professional, and yet my friends and clients say that I seem more helpful and easier to talk to than ever."

"More human, with problems like the rest of us," the stranger added. "I felt like that once—the more my life fell apart during that time, the closer people felt to me. Is that what you mean?"

"Yes, that's it exactly, and it helps to know I'm not alone in feeling this way," Roberta said with a weak smile.

There are times when we finally realize that our friends have been waiting to give to us or waiting to see if we are human like the rest of them instead of so perfectly put together. It seems like something in us literally has to break or be torn before we break down enough to let others into our lives. To let ourselves in, too, for we're the first person who got locked out of our carefully constructed lives.

That night, the psychotherapist discovered how long she'd been holding her life together and how, in a moment of haphazard movement, it could all fall apart. She was realizing that she would finally have to ask others to help her put her life back together.*

When people have accidents, there may be a lot that neither they nor you are aware of underneath the surface. Even accidents that don't seem serious can bring back memories of the tender loving care people did (or didn't) get in the past. If they aren't comfortable asking for help, acknowledging their love of independence may lessen their discomfort. Then you can offer to do something that's easy for you to do and might make it easier for them to

*Richard Carlson's book *Don't Sweat the Small Stuff . . . and It's All Small Stuff* is a helpful guide for responsibly coping with our own stress as well as helping people who have reached their limits.

accept. If you're the one who isn't used to letting others support you, you might begin by asking someone to do something that you'd be willing to do for that person if the roles were reversed—return library books, pick up a video, water the plants, drive to an appointment, or fix supper. It's all about taking one small step.

The Bear

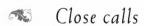 *Close calls*

WHEN MY BROTHER WENT TO HIS TWENTIETH HIGH SCHOOL REUNION, HE almost didn't make it back. His story helps us reflect on how to support people who have just had a near-miss. Even though they may walk away from their close call without so much as a scrape, we learn that the effects of those split-second moments can change their lives—and ours.

When my brother called to let me know that he'd returned, I asked, "How was the reunion?"

"Fine, fine," he said, and quickly changed the subject to talk about the days he'd spent hiking by himself in the Blue Ridge Mountains. He mentioned virtually nothing about the reunion.

It seemed peculiar to me, spending all this time talking about walks in the woods. After all, the main reason for the trip was attending his high school reunion, not hiking through the mountains. However, my brother had trained me not to ask him questions like an inquisitive older sister and to just let him talk about what *he* wanted to talk about. So he kept talking about the hikes. Finally he told me about the bear.

"A bear?" I asked. "Well, it *is* the Blue Ridge," I manage to comment nonchalantly. When we were kids, we used to see them stopping traffic along the Blue Ridge Parkway when we'd go up there for picnics.

"So what happened?" I asked, "Are you OK?" Then he paused, not sure of how much to tell me. Big sisters can come on pretty strong when they hear something has happened to the "little" brother in the family. Here's his story.

    🐾 After hiking about three miles out along the ridge below the mountain, I was getting ready to eat some lunch. I'd decided to sit out on a flat, rocky ledge for the view. Before I unpacked my food, though, I wanted to take a picture of me being in this spot. Nobody was out there but me. So I was setting up one of those self-timed photo shots. I set the camera on an old tree stump and set the timer. I moved out toward the ledge with my back to the camera while I took off my pack. I turned around and started walking toward the camera to set off the timer, and that's when I saw the bear. It was a really big black bear—nearly three hundred pounds.

    He slowly came toward me on the ledge, blocking my escape to the trail. I froze—probably stood there for about forty seconds—it felt like ten minutes. I couldn't think about anything. It felt like time stood still. To the bear I looked calm, but I don't think I was calm inside. I could hear my heart pounding, but everything else around me was silent. I kept saying to myself, Don't panic. Look him in the eye. Be still and don't move. Then he came toward me. I didn't have anything to defend myself with except possibly the camera, which had a strap.

He was about twenty feet away from me, still blocking my escape to the trail, so I figured, What the heck? I'll walk forward a few steps and gently pick up the camera and take a picture, because nobody's going to believe this. As I picked up the camera, the bear stood up on his hind legs and sniffed the air. I got the picture and took another as he dropped down and went back to eating berries.

"Guess you got lucky," I commented.

The story wasn't over, though. The only way for my brother to escape was to get off the ledge and get back on the trail. To do this, he had to pass within about fifteen feet of where the bear was eating berries. He managed to walk by the bear and proceeded up the hill and away from the area. For a while he kept looking over his shoulder to see if he was being followed by the bear. He decided to pick up a rock and a walking stick just in case.

What he didn't know was that the bear was tracking him up the hill along the trail. He just couldn't see it yet. He turned around and saw the bear trotting up the hill behind him. The bear started moving faster. My brother felt trapped. Alone. No one knew where he was. He was simply hiking in the mountains like he'd done many times in his twenties. Getting away from it all. Thinking about life. No chatter with a companion. Just him, the air, the view . . . *and the bear.*

Suddenly, the bear rose up on its back legs, sniffed the air, and charged up the hill, stopping only ten feet away from my brother, pounding his paws in the dirt. My brother held up the walking stick in his left hand and held the rock in his right hand as he crouched into a stance. He showed the bear he was ready to defend himself, but the animal didn't flinch. For whatever reason, after a brief stare-down, the bear must have figured it had convinced my brother that it owned the berry patch and stalked off to find more berries.

After it was over, my brother told me that he realized he'd been as close to death as he could remember. He was once in the midst of a hurricane's terrifying 180-mile-an-hour winds. He'd been in a car accident. He had survived both of those situations. But this, this was happening slowly enough for him to be thinking about the moves to make—to be totally aware of what was happening in the moment

"So how are you now?" I asked, thinking to myself that it had been several days since he returned. Maybe he'd needed some time to come to terms with what had happened.

"Let's put it this way," he explained. "I've been a lot nicer to people since coming down off the mountain. I am taking my time to appreciate little things. The things that normally bug me don't bug me that much anymore. A lot of things that seemed like a big deal are now smaller problems that can be handled. After staring down a charging bear, these are pretty small things for me now."

People react differently when they've had close calls—whether it was nearly being in a car accident, a bomb scare, missing a flight that crashes, a foiled mugging or crime, almost falling off a high ladder, or the possibility of being diagnosed with a serious illness. Some go into denial and get right back to work and life as it was. However, some people's experience immediately causes them to see their lives differently. It helps if we let them tell us how different life looks to them. Even if their brush with death left them unscathed, they may feel changed in ways we cannot see. For them, it may be a wake-up call to dramatically change their priorities. They don't want us to make light of the close call. They don't want us to talk about our close calls. They *do* want us to realize that weeks, months, and even years later, they may continue to see the event frozen in time and wonder why it happened to them.

Fresh insight is exactly what my brother received two weeks after his near-miss when Gordon, a Fish and Game officer, offered this comment: "Tell your brother that he is very lucky. No, I don't mean lucky that he wasn't killed or maimed. He's lucky because very few of us come face to face with a creature of the wild alone on his turf. It is a rare and precious experience to be treasured." My brother told me that this single comment gave him a new way to see his encounter.

Weeks after my brother's close call, I started thinking about the families who had just lost loved ones, in a flash, when Swissair flight 111 crashed in the waters of Nova Scotia. I thought about how it might have been for our family if the call had been from someone telling me my brother had unexpectedly died. Plane crashes, near-misses on a highway, an encounter with a wild animal on a hike—reminders that we never know when or how the people we love will leave us. I realized that *we* need to take time to sort out our feelings when we hear that someone we know has had a close call. Until we take stock of our emotional state, we may not be able to be of much comfort because we're in shock, too.

After the Accident

Fears remain

Y OU'RE JUST GUN-SHY," MY FRIEND SAID WHEN I ANNOUNCED THAT I WAS canceling the visit that we'd both been looking forward to for months. I couldn't believe I was still nervous. Thinking to myself, After all these years, you'd think I'd be fine. That's actually what most people think, that you get over something bad when time passes. My story reminds us that for some people, their fears don't lessen with the years. Here is my tale:

> There's snow and ice on the ground today. Reminds me of when my car spun out on a patch of black ice one night and was totaled by a truck. It happened four years ago. Wasn't the other driver's fault. Wasn't mine. Freak of nature. Who would have known on that dry, moonlit night that there'd be a patch of ice? Car was crushed, and I wound up with a lifetime of whiplash. Wasn't scared though, not

then. Went right back to driving and didn't think of it. Accidents happen.

It wasn't until nearly a year later when another car hit me head on that my friends told me to stop and look at my life. Whiplash again. No big deal, I thought; went right from the crash scene to work with clients. But friends started asking, "What is it going to take to get you to snap out of your denial? To look at your life and unhappy marriage? To get out of your head and your intellectualized numbness. To wake up and feel?"

Perhaps for the first time in my life, I actually felt scared. It wasn't a familiar feeling. Never felt fear, probably because whenever anything bad happened, I always went right into action. Took care of things, clients, other people. No time to feel. *No fear.*

Looking back today, I think the accidents had to happen to help me be more like other people. Fear is normal. *No fear* isn't normal, though I think we grow up in a world where we're taught, "Don't be afraid." So we grow up thinking, I'll be strong. I can tough it out. No big deal.

Accidents raise a lot of questions. However, those of us who have been in accidents would caution you to avoid making your first question "Were you driving?"—The implied question being, was it your fault? If you think about it, what *would* you say if someone admitted he was driving or that it was his fault? Answering that question could be an awkward moment for you both. There's also the question we often get, "Were you hurt?" Even if we weren't, is our fear or pain any less? It can be helpful to say to someone, "How are you doing now?" or "Can I drive you?" or "Would you like to talk about it? And it's OK if you don't want to talk."

There are a variety of ways you can be a helpful resource to people who have been in automobile accidents. They include the following:

- Recommend a good mechanic if they have to get their damaged car repaired.

- Offer to go with them to retrieve things from their wrecked car. They may not think they need company, but those of us who've gone alone will attest to the fact that we're not prepared to relive the crash, which can happen when you're standing there with strangers looking at what was your car and unexpected emotions surface as you wonder how and maybe even why you survived the accident.

- Ask if they'd like company when they go to rent, lease, or purchase another car. It can be helpful to have someone along to evaluate options or negotiate a deal because they may not be up to it.

- Offer to pick up their kids or run errands if they don't want to or can't drive.

I talked to my neighbors about feeling foolish because I was too nervous to drive on a day when to everyone else the roads seemed fine. I was trying to come to terms with getting older, getting a little wiser, and maybe not needing to push myself the way I had in the past.

Jabbing her finger into the air as she talked about her brush with a head-on collision, my neighbor said, "Look, when you get older, you see that the margin of safety in life may be a little less than the way it looked in your twenties and thirties. There were no margins in your twenties; you were invincible."

"Years ago, I wouldn't have given a thought to worrying about driving," I said.

"Bingo," my neighbor chortled. "You just didn't think about it then. Now you do, and that's fine; there's nothing wrong with growing up and expressing your feelings."

The gift that my neighbor gave me was her appreciation that memories of trying times don't leave; they just settle into their own middle age. By light-heartedly yet compassionately acknowledging my self-consciousness, she made it more acceptable for me to feel wary that what had happened to me before could happen again.

A Cry for Help

Responding to attempted suicide

THE MESSAGE ON THE ANSWERING MACHINE WAS CRYPTIC: "I NEED SOME help in knowing what to say. Please call me back."

When I called my longtime friend, her voice sounded determined. "What do I say to my nephew?" she asked. "He tried to kill himself two nights ago."

I took a deep breath and said I wasn't an expert on this. "I know that," she said, "and I've spoken with the Samaritan suicide hotline, but I still want to talk with you."

My friend had done exactly what professionals suggest: get help yourself to learn more about suicide and to learn what resources are out there for you as well as for the person you want to support.* In my friend's case, the hotline

---

*There is no intent here to provide expert professional advice on counseling someone who is thinking of taking his or her life or who recently attempted suicide. This story is an example of how to be sensitive to what you may not be able to imagine feeling yourself. I am not

counselor helped her understand how to be more open-minded and less reactive in listening to her nephew.

She'd written a draft letter to send to her teenage nephew. She'd learned that among the problems he faced was being tormented by bullies. She told me that her nephew was at a special youth facility and that he and his family were receiving professional counseling about his suicide attempt. She didn't want to try to counsel him, but she did want help in knowing how to let him know that she cared.

I read the draft of her letter, and much of it was wonderful. Caring. Loving. She was sad about what had happened to her nephew. However, she also emphasized how much she and her girls would have missed him if he had succeeded in taking his life. I sensed that an unintentional result would be to possibly make her nephew feel guilty about how his actions hurt others. So I paused to carefully ask her some questions so that she could see this for herself.

I told my friend that I had read the letter. Then I took another deep breath and asked her how she was feeling right now. She sounded angry to me. She realized that she was. Not at her nephew but at the circumstances in his life that had led him to want to end it. I said, "It's important for you to know how you feel before you try to connect with him. Realize that you are feeling angry, probably not only for him but also for things that may have

---

a professional suicide prevention counselor; however, I know that we all have the potential to provide comfort and clarity to the people we care about, based on our ability to hear them— to try to understand. If you have any doubts about how to be with someone who has been in this situation, please go to your Yellow Pages, look up "Suicide," and call a professional or the Samaritan (or your local) suicide help line or community mental health center right away. Before you intervene in any way, be sure that individuals with suicidal feelings are obtaining care from professionals specializing in suicide prevention and recovery.

happened in your life that made you feel hopeless even if you didn't try to end your life."

"Yes," she said, "that could be so."

Then I told her that lots of times the first instinct when talking to individuals who have tried to commit suicide (or are thinking about it) is to tell them how much you would have missed them or how much they have to live for. I've learned that in the early stages of either thinking about killing yourself or in the aftermath of an unsuccessful attempt, you aren't ready to hear someone tell you what you have to live for. You don't believe it, so you can't hear it! Then, when people start trying to tell you how much they would have missed you, you feel either guilty or defensive. You think to yourself, That's your problem; it's my life. I'm not here to make your life better.[†]

It's possible that individuals who are considering suicide have reached a point, for whatever reason, where they can't see a light at the end of the tunnel. It doesn't have to make sense to you or anyone else. We know that they have a purpose in life, have a lot to live for, and are loved. Here's the thing: they may agree with us intellectually, but they don't think it matters anymore. They feel numb, dead, and so shut down inside that our words can't easily get through the barriers.

One of the things the suicide prevention centers teach their volunteers is the same concept they teach in hostage taking: try to connect. Try to create comfort for these individuals, build trust, get inside of their head, offer nonjudgmental listening, let them know you understand them. Just be someone

---

[†]There are many resources for learning more about what motivates people to consider suicide, including *The Enigma of Suicide* by George Howe Colt and *Suicide Prevention, Intervention, Postvention* by Earl Grollman. (See Resources for additional information.)

they can talk to about how hopeless and heartless their life seems. Let them know that you will be there with them as they go through the struggle to get to the other side. You need to come to terms with your reactions to realize that for some, it's not that they didn't have anyone to turn to or that they couldn't ask for help; it's that they felt that not even you or their best friend or spouse or lover or child—no one could help them when to them, their life no longer seemed worth living.

At the close of our call, I told my friend, "Think about what your nephew can hear at this moment. Don't try to tell him all the things you want to tell him right now. Think of the one thing that he would be willing to believe. It could be the first step toward helping him respect himself enough to want to live a little longer. Don't make him feel guilty, even by nicely saying how much you would have missed him. Not yet. Tell him later."

Here is an excerpt from the revised letter she sent to her nephew:

> Dear . . . ,
>
> I wish I could listen to your thoughts right now.
> And know what you're thinking. And what you're feeling. I wish that you could have someone to speak with, who bears no judgment. Who can listen unconditionally to what you would say. I wish I could be that someone.
> I understand that you slit your wrists the other day. I've never told you what to do, or not to do; and I'm not about to start now. I have to wonder, though, if such a permanent "solution" is the only one to the conditions you face. I have to hope that time will bring changes to your life and hopefully to our culture.

You know I also hate the oppressive nature of our culture. *And* I know there is an opportunity for people like you and me to stop tolerating bullies. To stop tolerating an oppressive culture. I don't know what to do, but I do know that I need people like you to work with.

You've also been a very good cousin to my daughters. They have no brothers. I hope you will choose to sustain your life. Even if that is a day-by-day choice, I hope you will make that choice. And if you are ever considering taking your life, I hope you will call me and talk. I promise to listen. If you want to see options other than what's apparent, ask me. I'm wickedly good at thinking outside the box. And it's always easier to see out than to see in. If you ask, I'll respond. I won't impose. I don't know what you want or need. But I want you to know, I'm here for you.

I love you.

My friend approached her nephew's suicide attempt as a call for help, not a commitment to die. Today he is getting that help. Had his aunt assumed that his actions had been driven by a desire to die rather than an attempt to get help, it would have been much harder for her to provide the nonjudgmental listening her nephew needed.

Reflection

 # How to Be with Someone Who's in Pain

How do we sit in the presence of someone else's pain?

One of the greatest gifts we can give is to be with someone who is in pain. Since all of us have been in pain at one time or another, we know that it comes in many colors. There's physical pain. There's emotional pain. There's the fear of the unknown and the fear that the pain will never stop. There's numbness, which actually brings on the pain of feeling profoundly disconnected. Then there's the anguish we feel when we worry about the pain we think our pain is causing others.

What can we do to be with someone who is having a difficult time? Breathe. That's right, keep breathing. Think of the birth coaches, spouses, friends, and nurses who are being with a woman in labor—said by many to be among the greatest physical pains anyone ever bears. What are those helpers doing? Breathing with the mother-to-be to help her ride the waves of pain. It's so easy to do just the opposite when you are with someone who is hurting. Regardless of whether their pain is physical or emotional, we start holding our breath without knowing it. We tighten up our muscles. We try to hold ourselves together, keep our emotions under control. This may also be what the person you are trying to comfort is doing as well—trying not to let the pain show.

When we hold our breath, we lose touch with our ability to feel. The less oxygen we exchange, the less oxygen is supplied to refresh our cells and keep our blood circulating. We can tighten up in our body and our brain—hence the old advice when you are facing a difficult situation: take a deep breath. It literally restores your senses. Breathing softly and deeply can calm you, and your relaxed energy can create a sense of peace for the person you are trying to help.

Being with the spirit of others—which is often most vulnerable when they are in pain—means that we also have to be willing to let their pain touch us without fearing that it will overwhelm or contaminate us. A common healing meditation practice encourages us to "be willing to breathe in another's pain and breathe back your love and blessing."*

One way you can support people who are in pain—whether emotional, physical, or both—is to *allow their tears.* It's natural for us to want to end the tears, to say, "It will be all right; please don't cry." It can be hard for us to sit there feeling somewhat helpless as they are sobbing or even gently weeping. Yet their body is trying to move emotions out of its system—to release the healing that comes with tears. To let the pain literally flow. If you can, try not to rush for the tissues or scoop people up in your arms. Just let them know you are there; then, after a few minutes,

---

*The Buddhist practice of this meditation, known as *tonglen,* is beautifully described in Pema Chödrön's book, *The Places That Scare You: A Guide to Fearlessness in Difficult Times.*

offer a gentle touch or a shoulder without assuming their burdens as your own.

You or the individuals you are comforting may at different times regard pain as a teacher, a curse, a punishment, an injustice, or a natural part of being alive. Regardless of how people view their pain, it helps if you can appreciate their view. You can also keep asking them, or professionals, how to help them feel more comfortable. Sometimes, however, all you can do is help them bear it if nothing can be done to relieve the pain.

It is not our role to make the pain go away, much as we wish we could. Sometimes, out of a desire to express how much we care, we say things like "I wish it were me that this was happening to" or "If I could take your place, I would." These words can sound well meant but hollow to the individuals we're trying to support, because as much as you would like to trade places with them or somehow make their pain go away, the truth is that you can't, and they know it.

Perhaps we can say something like a friend said to me the other day. With tears in her eyes, she struggled to find a way to help me deal with an upsetting situation that had left me feeling like I'd been emotionally poisoned. She began by telling me how helpless she felt and said she wished she could do something for me. It hadn't occurred to me that watching me struggle was painful for her. Then, without knowing it at the time, she offered me a huge gift: "It sounds like the pain you are feeling is releasing toxins into your body that you might want to find a way to eliminate," she said slowly, with a little self-conscious hesitation. "I wonder whether it would help you at all to do what I've learned to do to flush the chemo out of my healthy organs."

I said it might help for me to hear her story. She then told me how she deals with the agonizing aftereffects of chemotherapy: "I visualize the chemo going to my cancer cells and simultaneously leaving the healthy organs such as my liver and kidneys. I sit quietly, meditate, and tell my body to do its work: fight cancer cells and release the toxins out of the healthy cells."

What was so healing about this conversation was that the friend who offered me the gift of her own meditation didn't tell me what I should do. She was *being with* my pain by letting me experience how vulnerably she was able to be with her own pain.

Trading places for a moment, what if you are the person who needs to be comforted but don't know how to ask for what you need? One step you can take with close friends or relatives is to let them know that instead of their uncomfortably ignoring the fact that something has happened to you, all you really want is for them to ask, "How was that test you got today; did it hurt?" or "Are you scared of getting into a relationship again?" or "I don't know what to do for you; I feel so helpless" or "Are you afraid of dying?" You can become so good at being strong or "handling" your pain that your friends don't know what you need from them or that you need anything at all. Until you can speak honestly about your fears or say what you truly need, you may keep people at a distance, unable to tell you the very thing you long to hear or unable to share what's going on for you.

    ❧ If you were suddenly diagnosed with a serious illness, how would you want others to help you? Would you play it close to the vest, or would you want a circle of friends to know what support you or your family might appreciate?

~ What do you think you would need from friends, colleagues, or family if you weren't able to take care of yourself for a while? Who would you ask for help? What might make it a little easier for you to ask for *and* to accept the support that you'd need?

~ During a time of recovery, what might be the difference for you between a cure and healing?

CHAPTER THREE

Healing Conversations at Work

You People Are Incompetent!

Turning angry customers into loyal fans

Wʜᴀᴛ ᴅᴏ ʏᴏᴜ ᴅᴏ ᴡʜᴇɴ ᴏɴᴇ ᴏꜰ ʏᴏᴜʀ ʙᴇꜱᴛ ᴄᴜꜱᴛᴏᴍᴇʀꜱ ɪꜱ ᴏɴ ᴛʜᴇ ᴘʜᴏɴᴇ yelling at you for a mistake you aren't sure was your company's fault? Do you let the person vent? Calm the person down? Patch up the situation as best you can to stop the yelling? Defend your company's right to investigate? Say you're sorry and do whatever you can to make the caller happy?

No matter how much experience you've had, it's hard to deal with angry customers without taking their verbal assault personally. Yet that's what Donna, the director of reservations for a major hotel, had to deal with one morning when she came to work. Her story of how she shifted her attitude—from reacting and defending to investigating and mending—offers insights into coping with customer snafus.

One of our biggest customers, a tour company, had booked a client into one of our two hotels. That's what their director, George, claimed when he got me on the phone. He was screaming at me right from the start. Apparently, his client, Tom, had tried to check in at our three-star property, only to be told there was no record of a reservation. Tom insisted he had a reservation, and although he had no confirmation number from us, he did have a piece of paper from the tour company saying that he was booked at our hotel. To make matters worse, our hotel was completely sold out.

George was screaming at me about how incompetent we were: Didn't we know how to run our hotel? How could we tell a guest there was no reservation? Didn't we know that reflected badly on George's company? What were we thinking? "Your hotel is going to comp the guest for two free nights for both rooms."

Part of me wanted to say, "Now look here, you've never had a problem with our company before. You can't assume it's our fault. There's no confirmation number, so just hold on there. . . ." But instead of doing my usual routine of defending the hotel, I paused and remembered the training our group had had about a week earlier. We did some role-plays about dealing with upset customers. The first thing we'd learned to do was listen. The second thing we'd learned was that when you start justifying or explaining your reasons for something going wrong, the customer just gets more upset— even if your company did nothing wrong! I decided to try to use the new tools instead of reacting and taking this personally.

I let George vent. He was really angry; nothing I could say was going to help or even be heard. After he unloaded all of his complaints, I took a few breaths and slowly said, "George, let me take care of your customer, check things out, and get back to you once I know what happened. We can work this out."

"Don't bother to call me back—just comp the rooms," he answered and hung up.

First things first. I made sure the guest was given a premier room at our four-star hotel around the corner. Then I investigated what could have led to this problem. It occurred to me that maybe the tour company agent had mistakenly booked the client into a nearby hotel with a name similar to ours. And indeed, that's what I discovered: the tour company had made reservations for the guest at a hotel with a similar name. At that point, I asked my counterpart at the other hotel if she would do us a favor and not charge the guest a no-show fee.

Armed with what I had learned, I decided to pause once again before calling George back. I knew I'd been right that we had done nothing wrong, but I didn't want this attitude to come across in my tone of voice. I also wanted to try to practice something I'd learned in my training a week earlier: to put myself in someone else's shoes. So I thought for a moment about how mad I'd be if I'd made a reservation for someone in my family, knew I had booked the rooms, talked to someone at a hotel, and then was told there was no reservation. I'd be mad too. And maybe embarrassed. So with that outlook, I called George back.

I wanted him to know that his client was happily relocated in two upgraded rooms at our four-star property. Then I told him what I'd learned. At first he didn't believe me and said, "Are you sure that's what happened?" I quietly told him that I had the paperwork from the other hotel and would fax it over to him. I noted that he hadn't been the one to make the reservations for his client—someone else on his staff had made the call. Suddenly George started apologizing, telling me that he was sorry he'd yelled at me for a mistake that his company had made. He admitted that his office was short-staffed and he was trying to do the work of four people. But, he added, being short-staffed was no excuse for being short with me.

I told him, "Look, mistakes happen. I'm glad we were able to put your client up in our other hotel and get to the bottom of what went wrong. Thank you for apologizing. I appreciate that."

What I learned in dealing with George and his client was that you never know what's on someone else's plate. In the past, I would have spent more time up front insisting that our company had done nothing wrong.

"What would have happened to your guest?" I asked.

"We probably would have gotten him a room at another hotel, but it wouldn't have been our hotel, and he wouldn't have come back." she admitted.

"And what about the tour operator?"

"Oh, he would have taken his business elsewhere," she explained, being candid about the cost of being right. As it turned out, the tour operator wrote a letter to the owner of the hotel telling him how impressed he was with the way the snafu had been handled. "I'll be sending you all of my business," he wrote.

Here are some things that employees should keep in mind to help them manage their reactions when a customer gets upset:

- It's more important to understand the situation than to be right.
- Take the time to step into someone else's shoes if you want to understand what went wrong.

- Even if you are right, would you rather be right or in relationship with your customer?

- Pause to get your breath when someone is yelling at you, because at first all you want to do is yell back, interrupt to explain, or fix the problem fast. A few deep breaths give you "breathing room" for perspective.

- When someone's venting at you, all you can do is listen. The person isn't ready to hear what you have to say until he feels he's been heard *and* understood.

- You don't have to admit that your company is to blame, but you can say that you are sorry it is happening.

- Do what you can to make things right for the customer while honoring the customer's dignity and your company's budget and principles.

- Once you know what went wrong, explain the cause of the problem graciously, giving the customer a chance to save face while acknowledging that we're all human and mistakes happen.

What was the most challenging thing Donna had to learn in handling difficult customers? "Oh, that's easy," she said. "To keep my mouth shut. To listen and let someone vent without needing to immediately defend my company. Since learning this way of dealing with customers who think we are to blame for every problem, we've seen a huge decrease in losses we'd normally incur. These days we listen to them first, investigate second, put ourselves in their shoes third, and then reconcile the misunderstanding."

When Staff Don't Get Along
The power of listening

"Iᴛ I ʜᴀᴠᴇ ᴛᴏ ᴡᴏʀᴋ ᴡɪᴛʜ Rᴏɢᴇʀ, I'ᴍ ᴏᴜᴛᴛᴀ ʜᴇʀᴇ!"

When employees don't get along, it can cost a company more than money. Workplace personality conflicts can erode someone's self-esteem and force managers to face an awkward situation. Logan's story shows that consciously applying the principles of healing conversation can build constructive relationships between people who think they are hopelessly at odds with one another.

One evening, Mark came into my office and announced that he'd "had it" with Roger. Roger had warned us that he was tough to work with, but we hired him anyway because we needed his knowledge to compete in an industry where things were changing dramatically. When Mark confronted me, my instincts were to do what I'd normally do: assume that I knew what the problem was, agree that

Roger *was* challenging to work with, persuade Mark to just tough it out, and move on. I was like a lot of managers—the last thing I wanted to deal with was personnel issues.

Although I wanted to get right down to solving the problem, which as a boss was what I thought I was expected to do, I decided to try something else instead. I started off by saying something so simple: "You seem pretty upset, Mark."

"You're darn right I'm upset," Mark said. "Roger treats me like a five-year-old!"

Then I hesitated. I asked myself, What is he really trying to tell me? If he's feeling that he's being treated like a child instead of a grown-up, perhaps he feels that he isn't being respected. So I said to Mark, "It sounds like you don't think he respects you."

Mark paused for a few seconds and slowly said, "Well, no, not exactly. It's not that he doesn't respect me. It's that he doesn't understand how much I've learned."

His tone had changed. He was more relaxed. That's when I got a valuable insight. Just sincerely trying to understand him calmed things down. For the first time, I realized how profoundly we all want to be understood. If I didn't get it right, he would keep clarifying what he meant. Instead of saying anything else, I decided to let Mark keep talking.

"Look," he continued, "I've made a lot of money for this company. You've seen my sales records. Don't you agree?"

I was tempted to agree but I stuck to trying understand. "Mark, it sounds as if you feel that you've learned what you need to learn and are ready to get back out on the road with the customers instead of being in the back office training."

"Yes, that's it," he said, "and Roger is too busy to even notice how much I've learned!"

Mark was beginning to see Roger in a new light. And I was beginning to see the problem in a new light. We were getting to the root cause of the problem, and it wasn't, to my surprise, Roger's personality. "So it seems that because he's so wrapped up in what he's doing, Roger wouldn't know that you're ready to get back out there and start selling the new products."

Mark paused again. Then he said, "You know, you're right, Logan. He hasn't had time to look at the progress I've made. It's up to me to fill him in. I think I'll go talk to him about my scheduling a road trip and see if he can help me plan it. I'm all set now. I'd like to go talk to Roger now. Will you authorize a sales trip?"

Logan's conversation took only a few minutes, but for him it was an epiphany. What he thought was the problem—a difficult yet talented employee rubbing another one the wrong way—wasn't the problem. Instead, by not rushing to agree with the angry employee and by not deciding to go off and lecture the difficult one, he realized that the problem was that the two employees weren't communicating. Roger didn't realize how much progress Mark had made, and Mark didn't realize that his nemesis had been too busy to notice that Mark had learned what he needed to learn and was ready to go back to doing his regular job (where in fact he went on to make record sales).

Executives are expected to take action; listening seems so passive. Logan's story demonstrates that hearing the feelings beneath the words can be the best, first response to conflict. As Logan discovered, people have an amazing ability to fix their own problems if we'll listen.

What if being a leader is about ensuring the quality of relationships—among employees, customers, and strategic partners or vendors? What if the role of a leader isn't about having the answers all the time—it's about being able to consciously sift through the conflicting currents of employees' reactions and misunderstandings? What if a leader's role is to be a bridge between employee differences, producing a caring environment where coworkers and the company both benefit? What if being a leader is having healing conversations—even at work?

Trading Places

Helping a colleague pause before jumping to conclusions

WHEN PEOPLE HAVE TROUBLE RECOGNIZING WHAT IS BOTHERING THEM, how do you help them see it? It's a challenge a lot of us can face at work when, from the outside looking in, we can understand what's amiss but our colleague only sees that he or she is right and everyone else is wrong. As in any situation where people are upset, how can you help them pause to find a fresh perspective without telling them what to do? As you "eavesdrop" on a coaching session with a manager, see if you can spot which of the healing conversation guidelines (presented in Getting Started) could apply if you faced a similar situation.

David was responsible for making sure that several key departments at the hotel he helped run did their very best. For him, their very best was as good as he would have done it. It wasn't unusual for him to lose both his temper and his patience when someone didn't measure up to his standards. One day, he saw employees wearing sneakers on the job. "Sneakers!" he said in disgust. "It's unacceptable. Just who do they think they are?"

I pointed out that the employees wearing sneakers had to stand on their feet all day staffing the guest reception desk. Eight hours a day. Standing.

"But it's against company policy," he told me. "There's no way we could ever get a four-diamond rating if the inspector caught our front desk people wearing sneakers while working for our hotel."

"I see. So what are you going to do about it?" I asked.

"Tell them to wear regulation shoes and be done with it," he said, quite annoyed.

"Well, do you have a clue as to why some of them are wearing sneakers when they know it's not allowed?"

"No, and I don't care, " he said, irritated at the idea of wasting any time trying to figure out why his people were doing something as *dumb* as wearing sneakers to work.

So we paused and I asked him if we could fish around for a while to see what might drive his employees to break the rules. "Imagine you are a front desk person," I started off as I laid out one scenario. "You've got to stand on your feet all day. You've been told that the company goal is to provide warm and friendly service to every guest. On your feet all day. No sitting. Not much moving around. Standing there. Being friendly. Got the picture?" I asked.

"Sure," he said.

"Now," I added, "put yourself in their shoes: why might you wear sneakers?"

"I wouldn't," he said, annoyed. "That's just my point. If I had their job— and I have done it before—I wouldn't wear anything but regulation shoes. Breaking the rules doesn't make any sense to me."

"Right," I said, "because you haven't stepped into their shoes. You are looking at it as if you stepped into their job wearing *your* shoes. You haven't taken the extra step to look at the situation as if you were them, not as if you were you doing their job your way."

"Exactly," he said, "and I can't imagine why anyone would do that." Then it dawned on him. There was no way, as a senior manager in this company, that he was going to get to the bottom of the real problem unless he stopped thinking that everyone should do it his way. As long as he held on to being right and seeing everyone else as wrong, he couldn't really discover what was motivating his people to break a rule.

In the end, he discovered that the reason they were wearing sneakers was that the pad where they stood didn't give them enough cushioning and left them with sore feet and backaches—making it difficult to be "warm and friendly" while checking in harried travelers. The solution? Rather than angrily prohibiting sneakers, he ordered a new, thicker mat. His people went back to wearing regulation shoes and truly felt that he had taken the time to see things from their point of view. He had finally tried to stand in their shoes!

"I thought that putting myself in another person's job and doing it the way I'd do it was what you did when you were stepping into another person's place. But if I do that, I haven't tried a new view at all—I'm defending mine and still blind to the other person's."

What do colleagues need you to be to help them see what they can't see?

- Someone who won't judge them as an unfeeling person.
- Someone who won't tell them they were wrong or rush to point out answers.

- Someone who appreciates that there are some (not necessarily obvious) reasons why they are having trouble understanding the situation.

- Someone who has compassion for their frustration. (For example, in this story, David couldn't see what he was missing until it was safe for him to admit that he had been trained to do things differently. Once he could say that, without feeling wrong, he was willing to take a fresh look at the picture—to at least be curious about what he hadn't been able to see. As a listener, when you give compassion to people who are feeling wronged, they can often then give it to themselves and then pass it along to others.)

If you are the one having a tough time understanding what's going on and don't have someone to help you sort things through, consider taking a few minutes to trade places with the person who is upsetting you. Taking this step before you deliver critical feedback can help you appreciate that you may not have the whole story. You could start your conversation by saying, "Maybe I'm missing something here. . . . This is what I'm seeing. Can you fill me in?" When you take the time to pause and acknowledge what you don't know, you're making it easier for employees to help you solve the problem rather than wasting energy defending themselves against your assumptions.

You Must Be Kidding!

🐚 *Giving and getting difficult feedback*

ALEX HAD A PROBLEM, ONE HE'D BEEN TRYING TO AVOID DEALING WITH FOR several months. His problem was Madeline, a competitive go-getter whom the company wanted to promote. The CEO was pressuring him to promote her soon, fearful that the company might lose her to the competition, and it couldn't afford to have that happen.

Madeline was fully expecting to be promoted. Clients admired her. In fact, her work was often too good. Colleagues felt that they couldn't compete with her. They complained about her sharp tongue, about how quick she was to criticize, and about her impossibly high standards. There was a feeling that when someone else was speaking in a meeting, she was thinking to herself, Oh, puleeeeze, get to the point!

Alex finally had to take action when several employees refused to work on Madeline's team.

ALEX: It took me months before I was ready to have the conversation with Madeline. What if I'm wrong about her problems? I wondered. What if she turns on me and starts telling me all the things I'm doing wrong as a manager? Or says, "Who do you think you are to criticize me?" Or says, "I quit!"

MADELINE: When my boss told me point blank what my supervisor had been subtly trying to tell me for a while, I couldn't believe it. I thought I was doing a great job and on my way to a promotion. Instead, I learned that several colleagues didn't want to work with me. I was devastated! Suddenly I was being asked to accept some serious coaching to change the way I operated. First I had to ask myself, Did *I* want to change?

ALEX: The hardest thing for me to say to Madeline was "You have a perception problem. Your colleagues find it difficult to work with you. Their perception is that you think you are better than everyone else. That's why you don't delegate—because you don't think that anyone can else do it the way you want it. You may not think that this is the way you are coming across, but the truth is that perception is reality. The question is, are you willing to work on it?"

MADELINE: The first time my boss brought up the subject of my management style, I didn't want to hear it. "Give me a break. Nobody can get the job done like I can. I don't have time to bother with all this. I'm too busy."

ALEX: I was also wondering whether the problems we were having with this high-performing employee were because of her personality or her lack of management skills. I knew it wasn't fair to tell her to change who she was—to become more like us—but for the sake of the company and morale, I had to tell her that she needed to adopt a more inclusive style of management—to be less self-centered.

MADELINE: I'll just quit, I thought. It would be easier than changing my personality. I wondered to myself, But is there any truth to what my bosses are saying about how I treat people? Am I impatient with friends? Family? Am I judging people all the time? Is there really a problem here with me, or are my bosses being too sensitive to people who just can't cut it? I was stunned when family and friends said I was that way with them, too.

Get real, I said to myself. I guess you need to learn how to adjust your style—of being impatient and outspoken—without coming across as someone who doesn't want to listen to other people's ideas. My bosses wanted me to see how my actions affected the growth of others. My biggest challenge wasn't just that I needed to learn to listen; I had to *want* to listen to others in the first place.

Madeline's bosses gave her the choice to decide if in the interest of getting promoted to director, she would be willing to adopt an even more powerful way of achieving success by being more considerate of others. They gave her specific communication skills to develop, including listening to others' ideas without judging that hers were better, being more patient and considerate in providing feedback, teaching junior staff how to get the job done right instead of just doing it herself, and setting her ego aside to empower others to take the lead more often.

ALEX: One of the most important things we learned was that we, the management, were partly responsible for setting up some of the dysfunctional working conditions that fed Madeline's problems. She needed a supervisor who was skilled in teaching young managers how to delegate and to be part of a team.

MADELINE: My bosses were telling me that my staff and others needed a pat on the back and a chance to learn. But I did, too. However, I didn't have bosses who modeled that well, and I'd picked up some of their bad habits. I appreciated that my bosses were open to discovering some of the reasons I acted the way I did, instead of just making me feel that I was wrong and needed to be fixed.

After months of vigilant coaching by peers and what she called "soul searching"—hard introspective work that required her to treat caring about others and learning to listen as her primary job—Madeline began to notice a difference. So did her colleagues and her family.

MADELINE: We were on deadline to submit an expensive graphics package for a client. The team member who had done the work brought it to me for review. It was awful—nowhere near what I'd expected. In the past, I would have blown off the employee and done the work myself, wondering how she could be so incompetent. This time I paused to ask her, "Have you ever done this kind of project before?" She explained that she hadn't and was glad I'd asked her. We spent some time going over what needed to be changed and why. She told me that it helped her to see how to do it right and that next time she'd be able to do it right the first time.

Perhaps the most satisfying evidence that I've changed came recently when I was talking to my dad about his own frustrations with work. After we had talked, he looked at me and said, "A while ago, I didn't think that you could have sat there and listened to me. You would have tried to fix me or solve my problem. You've changed, Madeline, and I appreciate how you can listen to me now."

Being told that she was too hard on people at work was a wake-up call for Madeline. She had to face that what had appeared to be a problem at work was really a problem with how she was living her whole life—on and off the job. She had to learn that getting the job done wasn't just about getting the job done well and fast. It involved becoming aware of how other people were feeling. She'd never taken the time for that in a conscious way before.

ALEX: The most valuable thing I've learned is to have these kinds of healing conversations earlier in an employee's career. Instead of people turning on you in anger, I find that they respect you for telling them what the problem is and whether there is anything they can do to improve. I've stopped looking at people and hoping that things will work out somehow. Now I can see people for who they are; if they want to change they will, and if they don't, then it's all for the best that they move on.

If you want to give employees "hard to hear" feedback so that they are able to listen past their initial resentment, these healing conversation guidelines can help:

- Show up when it's awkward—acknowledge your own discomfort about breaking the news.

- Pause—be aware that you may not have the whole story about the employee's situation or behavior.

- Be there over the long haul—appreciate that it takes months to break in a new habit.

- Be a helpful resource—offer coaching and outside perspectives.

Plant Closings and Pink Slips

Taking away their jobs but not *their dignity*

TELLING PEOPLE THAT THEIR JOBS ARE BEING ELIMINATED, FOR WHATEVER reason, is one of the hardest conversations any of us can face. How do you get up the courage to tell people the awful truth and yet respect them at the same time? Ed's company staked its future on the way it answered that question.

Years ago, I was a senior manager at a company that lost its way as it grew. When we started out, we'd been a company that cared about our employees, but all that changed when the new CEO adopted policies that treated people like tools, not like human beings. When I started my own company, I knew I never wanted that to happen on my watch. That's why we developed a set of values to help us treat people well, no matter what happened. But recently, when I was facing a plant closing and layoffs, I almost lost my way. I only got back on track when a courageous employee asked me a killer question.

Because of a downturn in the telecommunications industry, we were going to have to consolidate manufacturing. That meant shutting down one plant and moving all of our operations to another one, three hours away. While we wanted all of our employees to move with us, being realistic, we knew that most of them probably wouldn't make the move. I was worried about meeting our delivery deadlines for customers, worried about maintaining a quality product during a time of understandable upheaval, and concerned about what this news would mean to our employees—many of whom were like family to me.

There was no way I wanted to tell them any of this until I had a plan all worked out. But Julie, my personnel manager, had a different plan. She asked me, "Ed, would *not* telling them be a way to respect them?" She was reminding me that months earlier, we'd promised to tell employees the truth when they'd asked whether we'd be closing this plant. We'd told them we'd let them know when we had made a decision.

Suddenly I knew there was no way I couldn't tell them, even though I didn't have the details worked out. I just didn't know how. I hate telling people bad news that would mean the end of their jobs because there's a part of me that feels like I've failed them somehow even if I know it's the right business decision. So I was looking for a way to avoid telling them face to face. Maybe a memo?

Julie asked me how I felt about what was happening. "Just awful," I told her. "After all, I hired most of them. They've done nothing wrong. We're just going through a slowdown in the industry. I think the world of them. But the best thing for us to do to make it through is to consolidate operations and save on overhead." That's when she had the courage to get tough with me. "Then tell them the truth and tell them how you feel—I've seen you do it before, and you can do it now," she insisted.

Right up until ten minutes before I was supposed to speak to the employees, I still didn't think I could go through with it. I'm not sure that I would have if Julie hadn't come up to me once again and said, "Tell them the truth—from your heart. You can do it." I had a hundred excuses for not talking to them until I had a detailed plan. And I still didn't know how the work would get done when I was giving everyone advance notice that most would lose their jobs. I knew that this wasn't the conventional way you did business in Silicon Valley and didn't know whether we would be able to make this complex shutdown and transfer work.

When I broke the news, I was choked up, and everyone knew it. They'd certainly never seen me, their CEO, that way. I'm a classic, confident, Harvard Business School grad who's been trained in the "never let 'em see you sweat" rule of leading a company. By telling my employees how difficult this was for me, knowing that most would be losing their jobs, they knew that I valued them. We announced that we had three months to get the transfer made, and we gave everyone the option to relocate. Later, when we got the details of the plant closing worked out, our operations manager began a "carpe diem initiative," enrolling everyone in the concept that if they were going to come to work, they might as well do their best and be proud of it—seize the day until the last day. And they did—meeting all of our customer deadlines, too.

As difficult as it was for me to face the employees that day—to talk to them, to take their questions, and to be with them one-on-one afterward—I realized that I didn't *want* to run a company based on distrust. I wanted to run a company based on a fundamental belief in caring about and trusting in our employees. If our company's values are that we believe in telling the truth and respecting people, then we'd have to do that in the bad times as well as the good. As it turned out, many of the employees told us that the way we treated them during this time made them want to work for us again if we ever reopened the plant. That was the best thing anyone could have said to me.

The essence of healing is awareness in action. Julie's awareness helped her boss have a courageous conversation that day with his employees in a number of ways:

- She didn't judge him for being afraid of not knowing what would happen when he spoke to employees.

- She had compassion for his concern that he would lose control of his emotions and not look like the "got it all together" leader he thought people needed him to be.

- She didn't insult his intelligence by telling him what to say or that it would be easy.

- She did what anyone should do when people are feeling overwhelmed by the present difficult situation: remind them of their past achievements.

Trapezes
❧ *Being laid off, fired, or acquired*

IT'S NOT FAIR, WHAT THEY ARE DOING TO THIS COMPANY. I LOVED IT HERE. IT was the kind of place where I felt I could spend the next ten years. We were like family. People you could trust. People you admired. A boss who believed in you. I can't believe this merger has destroyed the place. The forced resignations. The people who haven't resigned, they're like me; they know they can't stay there much longer. It's killing us inside."

Sam spoke these words early one morning when she'd come to talk to me about redesigning her career and her future. She was upset about the way people were being treated at her company after a merger.

> ❧ I can't do it again. Put my faith and trust into working for a
> great company and then wham! I'm asked to start all over again with
> a merged company that wants to change everything. So even if I go

along, then this new company could be taken over by a company with totally different priorities and principles.

You know what I can't stand? I can't stand it when friends come up to you and ask, "So what do you want to do?" As if you can easily answer this seemingly simple question. Or they'll ask if you've got an updated résumé they can pass around. I know they are trying to be helpful, but right now I'm mad and I feel betrayed. I'm not exactly in the mood to take job interviews at the moment, even though I know I'll have to go that route soon. How do you ever get your mind turned around enough to even care about another company when something like this happens?

Every day, people are changing jobs. Some leave because they're fed up, bored, have a better offer, or are ready for a change. Some are laid off or are fired or retire early. Some want to get a new job right away because they need the income or they can't stand being without a schedule, colleagues, staff, a sense of accomplishment, fringe benefits, and the feeling of being part of the working world. Others take time to consider their options. Those options can include thinking about different ways they could earn a living, make a difference, learn something new, teach, have an adventure, or do something they've always wanted to do.

If you're trying to support people who are going through a job change or who, like Sam, are wondering whether to quit, one thing you can do is be a sounding board and a resource. In the beginning, don't try to talk them into or out of anything. If they ask you to help them with a résumé, be candid and patient. Often people don't know how to explain their accomplishments in a way that others can understand. If they want to dream for a while about totally different career or noncareer paths, don't panic. That's healthy and could lead them to identify what their priorities are in a new job or in their life. They may seem lost, stuck, or overwhelmed because it seems impossible to start over again at their age or in their line of work or in the town where they live. It's a good idea to let them express those feelings—or if they'd rather clear out the basement, just let them. Mostly, people need help identifying small steps that they can take in new directions. Even if you can see exactly what they should do next, they may not be ready to take that step yet.

Then there's this advice from a former Harvard psychology professor who made his own transition to being a CEO: "You can't go out and start a new job when you haven't let yourself be angry and sad about the one you are leaving. It doesn't matter whether you quit, were laid off, or were fired. You need to have a wake for your old job." He helped me realize that ending a job was a lot like going through a death and that we need to say goodbye, grieve, even have some symbolic ending for that period of our life.

If you're trying to support someone who is going through the loss of a job—your husband, your wife, a friend, a colleague, or a sibling—doing the following can help:

- Pause and feel what's going on for *you*. You may feel angry that the person didn't take your earlier advice to find a better job ages ago. You may be concerned about your own welfare now that loss of income is a reality.

- Get curious and imagine what might be going on for this person, even if you don't think you'd be feeling the same.

- Remember, even though taking the initiative might make us feel good, we haven't been asked to fix the upset, find a new job, or get the old job back.

Not knowing how to support a loved one who has lost a job is a crucible in itself.

William Bridges's book *Transitions* is a wonderful resource for spouses and family members to read as a way to support a person whose career is in flux. The author teaches a productive way to deal with change. You can either go through life by moving straight from point *A* to point *B*—in which case all you do is get from one place to another. Or you can pause long enough in the "know-nothing" zone to allow your transition to generate a transformation. The transformation occurs because you take the time to become more aware of your gifts, your potential, and your desires.

One way to see job change is as a transformation through transition. It can be a messy, difficult process that makes you doubt your abilities and dreams. It can be a time of ups and downs. However, if the person whose job is up in the air can get some support from other people, it can provide the strength needed to let go of the past and reach out for the next trapeze bar. In the essay "Fear of Transformation," recently reprinted in the *Essene Book of Days, 2001,* authors Danaam and Danaan Parry describe the transition process using the metaphor of a trapeze. In essence, they say that for us to grow, we need to be willing to let go of the trapeze bar we're holding on to before we can possibly grab the new one swinging toward us.

Bad News at the Office

Crossing invisible boundaries

WHAT DO YOU SAY WHEN SOMEONE YOU KNOW, OR BARELY KNOW, GETS BAD news at the office? Do you cross the line of an employee-boss relationship? What happens if you let your guard down? Can you be a client and also be a friend? Can you be close one day and professional the next? Christine's story helps us see what happens when you realize that regardless of what title you have at work, you are a human being first.

I didn't expect to get the call at work. When the doctor said she had bad news, I'm not sure I heard anything she said after the word *cancer.* I just sat in my office feeling numb for about twenty minutes. Then the phone rang. It was a client, a broker. I serve as the landlord for a commercial real estate management company, and he and I had been negotiating lease proposals for a building that was soon to be vacant.

"How are you?" he asked.

To my complete surprise, I burst into tears. I sobbed and sobbed, telling him that my doctor had just called to tell me that I had breast cancer and needed surgery immediately. I couldn't believe I was telling all of this to a client, someone I did business with over the phone but hadn't ever met. He expressed his sympathies, and somehow I was able to get myself together enough to ask him how I could help him.

"Oh, no," he insisted, "we'll talk another day."

"No, really," I answered, "I'd like to talk about work right now. Please, let's talk about why you called." So we proceeded to discuss business. I needed to still think of myself as a person who could work and think and help people.

Three days later, I got an unexpected letter in the mail from this same client. He had sent me a two-page, handwritten note telling me a very personal story about what happened when cancer showed up in his life. Here is what he wrote:

Dear Christine,

I'm sorry to hear about your situation. Let me tell you a story.

In 1969 my father died of lung cancer. Three years later my mother was diagnosed with uterine cancer and was scheduled for surgery. I went home prior to my mother's check-in for surgery to be with her for what could be the last time. The night before she was to go to the hospital I got into a bad traffic accident (single vehicle in the mountains). I was very lucky, but the end result was a Frankenstein face—50 stitches—skin ripped off—a real horrifying visual mess.

Wanting not to freak my mother out, I opted to talk to her on the phone rather than let her see her son ripped to shreds. I didn't see her for 30 days until my face (one side at least) cleared up. When I finally saw her, she looked like a concentration camp victim—elbows bigger than arms—knees bigger than legs. I walked out of the hospital in tears because my mother looked just like my father did days before he died. I was sure she had only days to live. I was going to be alone. I was devastated. But there was something I was unaware of and hadn't counted on. It was her attitude and spirit. No cancer was gonna kick her ass. The doctors put her through it all—the knife, radiation, rerouted her interior plumbing, fried a kidney and fixed it so she could pee in a bag attached to her hip. They pasted, stitched, and glued her back together.

It's 31 years later and at 88 my mother is in more superior physical condition than people 20 years her junior.

I hope this story isn't too much. I mention all this because I know one of the biggest contributors to my mom's survival and recovery was her attitude and spirit, and as near as I can tell, you have those qualities in abundance. Your procedures will be a major inconvenience and a fight, but I am confident you'll kick ass and take names.

Good luck. Talk to you soon.

I called him up to thank him for his letter only to discover that ever since sending the letter he had worried that he might have offended me. He was concerned that maybe by being so personal he had crossed some kind of line in our working relationship. I told him that to the contrary, I was very touched by his gesture.

During the weeks I was waiting to have the surgery, I began to worry about my ability to do my job. Suddenly I realized that negotiating leases wasn't that important. I liked my job and was paid well to do it but feared that I wasn't giving it my best because now it was clear that there were more important things in life than my job. Fortunately, I had the surgery very soon after the diagnosis and was able to return to work with a new perspective: It's not that the job is what is so important—it's what I bring to the job. Because of the cancer, and the way clients and total strangers helped me through it, I've realized, more than ever, that we aren't our roles. We're human beings first. I think that looking at people this way has made me an even better employee because today I know that when I'm negotiating with a tenant, I take a lot more into consideration than the fact that he or she is just another person on the other side of the table.

Sometimes when people get bad news, they don't want to hear your story. They need you to hear their story or to listen to their fears. However, this story shows us that you can sincerely share something that happened to you in a way that might give strength to someone else. It also shows the importance of timing and respecting a person's privacy. By taking the time to handwrite a letter and then waiting a few days, giving her the chance to receive his thoughts in private, Christine's client showed consideration of her feelings and a respect for the fact that he didn't really know her well.

As Christine realized, what matters most is that we remember that on the other side of the phone, table, computer, or letter is someone who is more than a job title or designated workplace role. It's a human being with whom we can have a healing conversation if we remember that both of us are more than our jobs.

Celebrating Life

🦎 *Asking a coworker for help*
with a family dilemma

Hᴏᴡ ᴅᴏ ʏᴏᴜ ᴀsᴋ ᴀ ᴄᴏʟʟᴇᴀɢᴜᴇ ʏᴏᴜ ᴅᴏɴ'ᴛ ᴋɴᴏᴡ ᴡᴇʟʟ ꜰᴏʀ ʜᴇʟᴘ ᴡɪᴛʜ ᴀ family matter? That's what Kim managed to do one day at work when she asked a coworker to help her navigate the uncharted waters of loss. Her story reminds us that colleagues can share more than the fact that they work for the same company.

> 🦎 As the anniversary of my father's death approached, I was search-
> ing for a way to honor him. It had been eleven months since he had
> died of brain cancer. I can't remember how our conversation started,
> but in the course of getting to know a new colleague, I learned that
> she had lost both parents. I asked her how she gets through the
> anniversaries. She suggested that some people find comfort in cele-
> brating a person's life on the anniversaries rather than dwelling on
> mourning the person's death. She explained that's why some people

plant trees on such anniversaries as a symbol of everlasting life. She gave a few other suggestions as well, all of which were very helpful and thought-provoking.

The thing about my father was that he was never very fatherly to me. As the youngest of seven children, with four much older brothers, I think I never really needed my father to be my "father" because my brothers were always competing for that job. Instead, my father became one of my best friends. We shared all sorts of common interests, especially sports. We biked together, swam together, played tennis together (I taught him to play tennis when he was seventy). Just by letting me talk about him, my colleague helped me realize that I desperately needed to do something that represented my father's life, because for me that's what he symbolized—life!

I called my mother and siblings, and they agreed that planting a tree was a great idea. We arranged for the tree to be planted in a beautiful local park. The tree was to overlook the water and a boathouse, both of which were dear to him, sailor that he was. Although there was some question as to whether this young tree would survive in a spot subject to constant onshore winds, I knew that the spot we chose was where it had to be. The wind was imperative in honoring my father.

Months later, I miraculously learned that I was pregnant. I say "miraculously" because I had been told not long before that it was impossible for me to have a baby. I didn't connect the timing with the planting of my father's tree until the five-month sonogram, when the technician calculated that my conception date had been October 10. That was the day we had planted the tree!

When my daughter was about twelve months old, we began trying for a second child, but owing to the same medical problems, we
were unsuccessful. I prayed to my father and to God. As October 10
approached, an incredible calm came over me. I said to my husband,
"This is when we are going to conceive." My second child was born
nine months later on his sister's second birthday. Today we have
three children. I'm not sure any of this would have happened if it
hadn't been for a thoughtful colleague who was willing to listen and
to let me into her life, too.

Our workplace family can be a resource to us in ways we may not realize.
Kim unexpectedly found comfort in talking to a colleague she didn't know.
Supporting a colleague who is going through one of life's passages—such as
commemorating the life of a parent—isn't about knowing someone's family.
It's about being comfortable enough to ask a colleague to tell you about her
personal life, with gentle questions: "Tell me about your father. What was
important to him, and how did he share his life with you?" Letting Kim talk
about those memories helped her family discover a tribute that was just right.
If asked to tell your story, letting others know that the bewildering experience
they're going through is a journey you've taken as well can lift their spirits in
ways you'd never imagine.

I Just Wanted to Let You Know I Cared

❧ *Consoling an employee*

My ASSISTANT IS COMING BACK TOMORROW, AND I'VE BEEN TRYING TO figure out what to say to her when she walks in. Her grandmother just died, and she didn't get home to visit her grandmother before she passed away. Maybe it was my fault that my assistant didn't get back to visit. We were trying to work around some schedules so that she could take time off. Relatives hadn't told her that her grandmother was so close to dying—they only said that her health was failing.

"I'm sitting here realizing that this isn't about me and how I feel. It's about my assistant and what I can say to her. I've actually been sitting here wondering, do I ask her, 'So how was the funeral?' Then I think to myself, What a dumb question—I'm not asking for a movie review! Do I ask her, 'So how are you feeling?' Gosh, what would I say if someone asked me that? No way am I going to tell you how I'm feeling, stupid! Do I just say nothing, wait a few hours, and then go talk about business? Help me out here—why is this so hard?"

This conversation took place one day while I was coaching senior managers. When I dropped by the sales manager's office, Maureen found herself telling me about the dilemma she faced with a member of her staff. We talked about how she could just tell the truth. When in doubt, it's a good option. I asked her if she could say something like "I don't have a clue about how you are feeling right now. It's not my place to guess, but if there's anything you want to tell me about the service or your grandmother or how you are doing, I am interested because I care about you. If you don't want to talk about it right now, that's OK, too. I just wanted to let you know I cared."

"Yes," she said, "I could tell her I don't know what to say because it's the truth. I'd like to be able to tell her that I feel uncomfortable or a bit awkward about this."

"Right," I said. "Chances are that most of us won't ever learn how to be comfortable in these situations of loss. It helps whoever you are trying to comfort when you can be honest about the discomfort you feel because you don't know what to say. They'll appreciate that you are being sincere."

Then Maureen added, "We're trying to get our employees to help us grow the company but do it in a way where we let them know they matter to us. Then something happens—they get in a car accident or go through a divorce or have a death in the family—and because we don't know what to say, we don't say anything or say something so bland that it doesn't let them know we truly care. We need help in knowing what to say and how to say it . . . and what not to say. Maybe we should talk about how to just listen to people and not be so uncomfortable with showing we care. Isn't that what it's all about?"

"Yes, "I answered, "and there's one thing I can offer you about what not to say when someone's grandparent dies. Many times, without thinking, we'll ask someone who has just lost a grandparent, 'How old was she?' Then we'll say something like 'Well, at least she lived a long life.' We mean well, but we don't realize that for someone who has just lost Nana or Grandpa, it doesn't matter how long they lived. What does matter is that a loved one is gone and a way of life and perhaps an oasis of comfort have been lost. That's why it can be so much easier to hear something like 'Do you feel like telling me something special about your grandma?' Or you can ask, 'Did you two have certain things in common?' Questions like these let people pause to reflect and, if they are in the mood, tell you something about the person they still love."

There's another aspect to consoling an employee or colleague after a death. What do you say months after a death when your staff member or colleague is still struggling to come to terms with the loss of a friend or family member? Several people have asked that question after not knowing what to say to a colleague who, in the aftermath of a death, complains that work doesn't seem all that important anymore. That attitude might annoy you, especially if there's a lot of work to be done. However, if you pause for a moment, you may appreciate that this particular death is inspiring the person to ask, "What's *really* important in my life?"

Grieving people may feel that their life hasn't added up to very much. You might also hear about dreams deferred or passed up altogether. You might find yourself quietly reminding them, without trying to convince them, of what you think they have done that has mattered to them, to others, or to the company. It's a normal part of the grieving process to have the death of one person make us reconsider what we are doing with the rest of our lives.

Grief has no timeline. You will have to balance the needs of your company with the needs of your employee as best you can. If you feel that a "nothing matters much anymore" attitude is compromising an employee's work, you may want to raise the idea of temporarily restructuring the person's responsibilities. You may suggest that the employee take time off to reflect on whether he or she wants to make significant life changes. Or your company may have a policy for extended leave should that be more appropriate.

We can make the mistake of thinking that after some period of time, a person should be "getting over" a loved one's death. However, each of us is different in the way we deal with death. The death of a friend can affect us more than the death of a parent. It can take weeks or months before the question of "What am I doing with my life?" begins to hit home. Helping grieving employees temporarily restructure their workload shows your commitment to maintaining a healthy work environment where personal troubles are not swept under the rug or gossiped about behind closed doors. Any one of us may find ourselves in their shoes one day, being unable to concentrate on work as we try to come to grips with what's important in our lives. We can only hope that if we aren't aware of how our ongoing grief is affecting others, our boss or colleagues would have enough compassion to help us find our way.

Honoring Paul Tsongas

Coping with death in the workplace family

Sometimes getting in touch with your feelings doesn't happen right away. What do you say when friends and family call to ask how you are doing after the death of a colleague but you aren't ready to talk yet? You want to respond to their condolence calls, but you aren't ready to explain to others what this person meant to you—perhaps because you are just realizing the immense difference your colleague made in your life.

On January 26, 1997, a man who did a lot to shape my life at a young age passed away. That man was former U.S. Senator Paul Tsongas of Massachusetts. At one time he had been my boss. I went to work for him at the age of twenty-three during his Senate campaign. That's where he taught all of us the immense power of trusting our instincts. When Paul died, a lot of friends called to ask how I was doing. I was too sad to talk much on the telephone right after his death, but several days later, I wrote a eulogy of sorts and shared it with friends and with his family.

🐚 In Honor of Paul Tsongas: *Living Life*

Paul Tsongas taught me about being committed to what you believe, even if it wasn't popular. He taught me that people in power could admit that they were wrong. And do it publicly. He taught me to be good to the people on your way up—you'll meet them again on your way down. He also taught me to have people around you who are smarter than you—that way you'll learn, and they can contribute, too. He never gave up, even when the odds were against him—like with the brutal non-Hodgkin's lymphoma that he battled with two bone marrow transplants. Even when he died last week, no one could believe it because he had beaten the odds by living years beyond what doctors had predicted.

His death, just shy of his fifty-sixth birthday, was an incredible gift of life. So strange that in loss, we gain insight and new vision. In her eulogy, his youngest daughter, Molly, told us that, while others will miss her dad the politician, she will miss the guy who loaded butter and jam on his English muffins, who embarrassed her in fifth grade one day when he showed up with trash bags for everyone to pick up the garbage around the school. Looking back, she now sees he was just trying to get her involved in making a difference. "In the end," she said, "I will just miss my dad."

His middle daughter, Katina, told us that it wasn't until days after his death that she realized why so many people thought her dad was amazing. She said she'd wished she had understood this when she was still able to tell him. A man who was closer to him than most was his friend, law partner, and campaign manager, Dennis. He told us he realized now that Paul hadn't been one of those heroes you respect from the history books. He'd been a living hero, and Dennis wished he'd told him that before he died. "I am glad, " he added, "that I did tell him I loved him while he was still alive."

Sometimes it's excruciating to discover who someone was only after that someone is gone.

I appreciated that friends were able to accept that I wasn't able to talk to them when they first called. The loss was too fresh, and the impact of his death was deep. It was important to reassure them that it was fine that they had called and that some other time I would be able to talk about it. This was a case where a healing conversation began with a caring phone call and was continued when friends were thoughtful enough to respond later to what I had written and sent to them. Several unexpectedly comforted me by telling their own stories about how the senator's way of living his life had inspired them.

I don't think I would have been able to understand my grief as well as I did if friends and family hadn't been willing to let me take the time I needed to consider what I'd learned from someone I hadn't worked for in a long time. People were able to accept that I was bewildered for a few days and understood that talking on the phone wasn't what I needed. If people you are trying to comfort aren't interested in talking much about their loss, one thing you can do is give them some time to reflect. You can also be vulnerable enough to write them about what difference you saw their colleague make in their own life.

Notes to Keep a Memory Alive

A letter to the children

HOW DO WE WRITE A SYMPATHY NOTE TO THE FAMILY OF SOMEONE WE worked with—especially if the family doesn't know us? Maybe they have no idea what their father, sister, mother, or brother meant to us. How much do we share, and what would comfort them?

Over the years, I've written lots of notes to people I'd never known but with whom I've shared a loss. The family of one of those friends asked me to include this note as a reminder of something they learned when their father died: When strangers share their experiences about the one who has passed away, we help keep the person's memory alive.

FOR THE FAMILY OF NORM NATHAN

When I came to WEEI/CBS News Radio to begin work at my first real job, I was fresh out of college. It was pressure city in that newsroom! Thirty news stories an hour and anchors screaming at you should you, the novice, be so inept as to fail to write up the news stories quickly enough so that the on-air person never ran out of copy.

There was one anchor, however, who seemed to know what it was to be a human *being*—not just a human *doing*. When he ran out of copy, he'd simply stick his head out the news booth door and politely let you know that he'd take more copy when you had it ready. Then he'd smile, knowing you were doing the best you could and engaging you in the team effort called "Steady now, we can get through this."

First jobs leave lasting impressions. Some leave scars. Some leave lifetime habits. For me, the opportunity to be part of Norm's world was a chance to be sculpted in a good way. To have the teacher's chisel wielded with humor, care, and grace.

We have all been blessed by Norm's ability to delight in simple things and simple people. And yet his elegant and gentlemanly way reminds me that he had a gift for knowing what was really important in life. Not *who* was important but *what* was important: friendship, sharing, teaching, patience, and a loyalty to values.

You all have my very best wishes as you find your own ways of adjusting to life and living with Norm's presence in new ways.

You don't have to be a writer to let family members know about why someone you knew mattered to you. Just tell them a story. We all have our stories. After all, many of us spend more time at work with that "family" than we do with our own. In contrast to the family our colleague lived with at home, we may see different sides to this person who was our boss, our mentor, our critic, or who maybe even saved our neck on occasion. When writing your condolence note, I'd invite you to consider sharing a story about a special day, a memorable moment, or something that this person taught you. Don't be shy about telling the truth or having a sense of humor. Let the words come from your heart. Whatever you write can provide comfort and insight for years to come.

Maybe It *Is* My Job—
Intentional Kindness

What do you say at work when a customer needs your help but is asking
you to do something that isn't exactly in your job description? Can you
remember a time when you needed the help of a stranger—maybe it was
a flight attendant, an insurance claims agent, a receptionist at the doctor's
or lawyer's office, a cab driver, or a store clerk—and you needed more
than a random act of kindness? You needed the person to go beyond what
he had been trained to do, to listen for more than what she had been
trained to hear.

Every day, men and women get up, go to work, and expect to do the
job they're paid to do. Some of us are in the so-called helping professions—therapists, healers, teachers, coaches, lawyers, counselors—and
we're expected to know what to do or say when someone is having a rough
time. We don't always do it right, but at least we know that being there is
part of our job.

But what if you are on the other end of the phone and your job is,
more or less, to get a job done? Maybe you're an insurance agent, and as

far as you're concerned, your job is to focus on getting all the information about the car accident as quickly as possible. Or what if your job at the phone company is to take one more order to shut down a household's phone service because the family is moving? No big deal, you think; just get the new address and forwarding number and you're done. Maybe you feel like your job at the moving company is cut and dried: move the boxes onto the truck as efficiently as you can. Or to sell the house at the best price if you are the realtor. Or you are the receptionist who has to get the patient checked in at the doctor's office and cope the best you can if the doctor is running late.

What happens, though, when the human being (customer, patient, client) on the other end of the phone or at the head of your line needs something more? Maybe it's not something you are trained to do. Maybe you'll have to bend a rule or talk to a supervisor to find a way to help with something you've never dealt with before. What will it take from you in that moment to go beyond your training or to do something other than what you'd do in a normal situation?

If we can take the time to care about someone, even though it may not look like it's our job, it can change the way that person feels about the company or organization—for life. That's how one company gained a new customer one day thanks to the kindness of a single employee. I'd never been particularly impressed with that company before and had even taken pains to buy services from its competitors, but after that day, it will have my business, no matter what.

I'd arrived at the airport in time to catch a 7 A.M. flight only to discover that it had been cancelled. I was alone, traveling with a lot of hastily packed boxes and bags, and had nowhere to go back to if I couldn't get on a flight that busy Friday morning. There were about two hundred anxious passengers being rebooked by three harried ticket agents. I was feeling pretty fragile; however, I decided to be optimistic about getting a seat. The truth was, my composure was hanging by a thread.

By the time I was rebooked on a different airline, there was barely enough time to find a porter and hurry half a mile to the next terminal to be checked in. The ticket agent there looked at my ticket and frowned. "We can't accept this. It's not signed over to us by the other airline," he said matter-of-factly. "You'll have to go back there and get it signed," he said, handing it back to me.

The plane was leaving in twenty minutes!

"Uh-oh," I muttered. "The agent who rebooked me said that she'd never done this before. She's new and normally just checked people in. The other agents were trying to help train her, but it was pretty frantic over there; no wonder she didn't know what to do."

"Well, you'll have to go get this signed," he insisted, and pointed in the direction I had just come from. That's when I nearly lost it. To him I seemed like another traveler with a problem. But it wasn't his problem. It wasn't his fault. I'd have to just handle it. But there wasn't enough time for me to haul back over to that other airline and no assurance that I'd make any other flight out that day. With my voice shaking, I explained to him that I was unexpectedly moving out of state. I had just ended what had become a difficult relationship and had to leave my home in a hurry. I had no place to go here in this city and needed to get on that plane. Could he please help me?

Suddenly, he dropped his official manner and softened. He actually looked at me as if seeing me for the first time—not just as another passenger with a stupid ticket problem but as a person. He took back the ticket, called the other airline, explained the problem, and asked the airline to send someone over immediately to authorize the transfer. Then, realizing that I might miss the flight because the gate was so far from the ticket counter, he called the gate agents and asked them, if necessary, to hold off closing the boarding doors for a minute or two because a passenger was on her way. Indeed, I was the last person on the plane. That day, this ticket agent went beyond his job. He lived up to his company's advertising slogan: "Fly the friendly skies."

No matter what you do for a living, you never know when you will have the chance to help someone in need. It may take a change in the tone of your voice; it may mean that you look into her eyes to get a sense that there's something wrong, because at first glance, she seemed fine to you. If you're on the phone, it may mean that you slow down the pace of efficiently asking your official questions to hear more than what she is saying—to hear what she is feeling. You may need to put her on hold or ask her to step aside while you check with a colleague or supervisor to get some advice on how to help in that particular situation.

Here are examples of professions that may unexpectedly be called on to be there with more than a stamp, an appointment book, a cup of coffee, or a file claim number.

- The accident claims agent for an insurance company who takes the time to appreciate how scared you are to drive again and how lost you feel without a car

- The flight attendant who doesn't make a fuss when you are crying but brings you some water without asking and quietly asks if there is anything he or she can do

- The movers who understand that you're getting divorced and that they need to be very careful not to take anything that belongs to your soon-to-be ex-spouse

- The bank teller who stops being "official" about the way she is closing out your account when she learns that your relationship ended or your mother died or you lost your job and have to move

- The doorman at the hotel who asks if there is anything else he can take care of for you while you are visiting your sick relative at the hospital

- The secretary who takes her own initiative to get the person you are desperately trying to reach to call you back

- The customer service agent who helps you extend your credit during an emergency, saying that he hopes everything works out and he'll be thinking of you

- The postal clerk who takes the time to understand how sad you are about the letter or package you are sending that day

- The ticket agent who does everything possible to get you the best fare when you have to get somewhere in an emergency

- The pharmacist in your new town who takes a break from filling prescriptions to give you the names of a few local doctors because you're suddenly sick and don't know where to turn

- Anyone in *any* profession who, after listening to you mention that you're going through a difficult situation, decides not to end the call with the perfunctory "Thank you for calling XYZ Company. Is there anything else I can do for you today?" but instead says something like "I'll be thinking of you" or "I'm sorry this is happening to you right now" or "I do hope that things get better for you" or simply "I appreciate that this is a hard time for you."

On any given day, we never know who will walk into our lives. They may need our help and not look like it at first. They may unexpectedly reach a breaking point when all we've unwittingly done is treat them the way we'd treat anyone—at first. We may trigger them because we don't know what's on their plate. They may not be polite or have it all together when they're asking for our help. They may be crying, angry, confused, or ready to blame us for something that isn't our fault. That's why it takes an ability to shift—to not take their reaction or the situation personally. At the same time, it helps if we can pause to realize that each person we're dealing with isn't just another customer, client, patient, or guest—each is a human being having a problem that is beyond his or her (and possibly our) power to handle initially. You can shift the energy between the two of you by acknowledging, "I'm sorry. I didn't realize what was going on for you. Let me see what we can do" or "It sounds like you have a lot on your plate. I'm not sure what's possible, but let me check out a few options."

Sometimes all it takes to lift our spirits is that someone noticed. We may ask you for help and you may be able to give it your best try. And sometimes we may not ask for help and your thoughtfulness can be a deposit in our fairly empty emotional bank account. Employees who take the time to care not only feel good about doing their job, but they also add to the folklore of their company in ways that spread goodwill. You'll have customers who tell stories like mine: "Can you believe how nice this ticket agent was to me when I didn't even have a ticket for his airline? I was transferred from a cheap seat on a competitor!"

- ❧ What keeps you from pausing long enough to wonder what might be going on in another person's world?

- ❧ How could you get curious about what might be on the other person's plate that is making that person's life (and maybe yours) difficult?

- ❧ What would you have to do for *yourself* to switch to a slower gear so that you can hear what others are saying, what they're not saying, and what they wish it was safe to say to you about whatever is troubling them at that moment?

CHAPTER FOUR

Transitions

Heart, Mind, Body, and Soul

We're Getting Divorced

Appreciating what you may not understand

O NE OF THE MOST AWKWARD CONVERSATIONS WE CAN FACE MAY OCCUR when someone we know tells us, "I'm getting a divorce." We may find ourselves caught in the middle of wondering what went wrong, not knowing whether it's really over, or silently asking ourselves, "What took so long?" As Will told me his story, I reflected on how others' reactions play such a major role in a family's capacity to heal. Or, as he put it, it is so important "to get the kind of support from people that would enable our kids to feel that they had parents *after* our divorce."

One day, my wife just looked up at me and said, "I don't want to be married anymore." The idea of divorce didn't even register for me—it wasn't a concept in my vocabulary of life. I didn't know that she was having an affair; all I knew was that she was unhappy. Every once in a while over the years, she would tell me that she was lonely. Because my work often took me away, I offered to spend more time with her. "That's not it," she would say, but then she couldn't tell me what I needed to do to fix it. So we went on living our lives, raising four incredible children.

My wife and I had spent eighteen months trying to work things out. Nine months into it, I found out she was having an affair. She asked for the divorce, but I said an affair didn't have to mean the end of our marriage. We could work it out. But she moved out anyway.

For months, I lived on an emotional roller coaster. I'd drive to work one day, hopeful that we'd work it out because something good had happened between us recently. The next day, I'd want to run into a bridge abutment because whatever I thought had started to come together between us had fallen apart. I tried to get my work done the best I could—after all, I had five hundred people reporting to me. But I wasn't prepared when the rumors started flying at work: People thought my mind wasn't on my work because I was having an affair with someone at work; others assumed that I was addicted to drugs; some thought I was ill. I had not wanted to tell them the details of what was going on in my private life. I never realized that without information, people would supply their own falsehoods. That hurt almost as much as my wife's affair. It was another betrayal of trust.

"It seems like everything was out of your control during this time," I commented. "What helped you make it through dealing with your wife, your kids, and your colleagues?" I asked.

Three things were key. First, I asked myself, When all is said and done, what am I committed to in this process? The answer was being with my children. Whenever I had to make a tough decision, I focused on doing what it would take for the children to feel loved and safe. That's why I eventually moved out of the house and had her move back in. I gave up my home even though my wife had an affair because it was more important that my kids not have the upheaval of moving. My friends didn't understand why I was being so accommodating, given the way they felt I'd been lied to by my wife. It took them a while to understand that my priority was my children.

Second, a therapist strongly encouraged me to read the book *Crazy Time: Surviving Divorce and Rebuilding a New Life* by Abigail Trafford. It helped me make sense out of the crazy-making times by showing me what stage of the relationship I was in—from deadlock to separation to shock and then anger, ambivalence, depression, relief into emergence of self, and more. The book gave me some reassurance I would make it through if I kept working on it and didn't get stuck in a particular stage.

Third, I started to take some responsibility for why my wife had become so unhappy. I stopped blaming her. I stopped thinking that she had done this to me. She hadn't done anything to me. I had a right to be angry, hurt, and bewildered, but I also had to admit that someone else was able to offer my wife something she didn't know how to get from me and I didn't know how to give at that time.

"What was the hardest part about the divorce process?" I asked.

❧ The hardest thing was to teach my friends and family to stop putting my wife down. I kept having to explain that while the affair wasn't OK with me, I understood some of why it happened. It didn't help when people said things like "I can't understand how she could do this to you" or "Why would she want another man?" I know they were trying to make me feel that I was the one who had been wronged, but their comments only made me have to defend her. Friends need to realize that it doesn't help you when they take sides—no matter whose side they take. The other person is still your kids' parent.

Will has taken away from this experience not just memories of its pain but also an understanding that he didn't have before.

❧ It's taken me ten years to understand why my marriage fell apart. My friends have stuck by me over the years as I struggled to answer difficult questions. Their support helped me learn a lesson that I found myself teaching my son recently as he began to confront some issues in his own relationship. "You're going to have to have some tough conversations with your girlfriend," I told him, "and not run away like I did with your mother. Your mom and I didn't learn how to have these conversations until years after our divorce, and if we had learned them earlier . . . who knows?"

When you're with people who are navigating the before, during, and after stages of divorce, here are some useful guidelines:

- Try to resist the temptation to finally tell them what you've thought all these years about their spouse. At least for now. They can say whatever they want to about their former spouse, but that's not true for anyone trying to comfort them.

- You may wonder why a couple ever married or how they even stayed together. They may be wondering the same things. Again, let them tell you that rather than telling them your opinion. If they're having second thoughts, don't panic. It's normal.

- Please don't say congratulations once the divorce is final. Maybe the parties are relieved that it's over, but not everyone feels that it's something that deserves congratulations.

- Please don't ask the newly divorced if they are dating. If they want to tell you, they will.

- You may be wondering whether they've gotten any insights into what happened and whether they're gun-shy about ever trying again. They're probably wondering the same thing. You could say something like, "I'm wondering what you're thinking, looking back on things." Then be quiet and listen. If they want to share any insights or fears, they will. If they don't, they'll tell you so.

Some of us find it hard to accept that we are "divorced." We don't want to check off that box on the many forms we have to fill out for health care, bank accounts, insurance, a mortgage, and so on. It feels like we are now a statistic with a stigma. Are we "single," "unmarried," "divorced"? It takes a while to adjust, not only to filling out those forms but also to filling in the emotional gaps.

Be a Friend, Not a Hero

Helping someone deal with verbal abuse

Be a friend, not a hero. That's what Albert had to remind himself one night when his friend Eve came to talk to him about her new boyfriend, John. She'd told Albert there had been some scary moments that had taken her by surprise. Their story is about helping someone make the transition from unconscious victim to survivor and beyond.

"I'm so confused," Eve told Albert, explaining that her boyfriend seemed nurturing and tender when they first met. "There's this other side that leaps out all of a sudden," she said sadly. "He'll get angry or sarcastic, putting me down for what seem like little things that I do or say. I don't understand what I've done wrong. Or sometimes he'll just get quiet and won't let me know why he is so angry. I feel like I'm turning myself inside out to do or say the right thing so that he won't get mad. I've never had this in a relationship before, and I'm not sure what to do."

"Tell me more," Albert said, knowing that he needed time to get a handle on his own reaction to her story. Alarm bells were going off for him: she could be in danger.

"One of my employees won a contest for doing the best job on a project," Eve explained. "The prize was to go to lunch with your boss. I told John about it and was very proud that one of my people had won. He had a fit: 'You're not going to go to lunch alone with another man!' I tried to explain that it was only a lunch and it was part of the award program. But he wouldn't hear of it. I was embarrassed to tell my own boss this, but I thought, OK, if it's so important to him, fine, I'll take someone along with me. But I knew something felt off-kilter about this. It's perfectly normal in business to have lunch with a male colleague."

"So it sounds like he likes to call the shots," Albert said, trying to help her hear what it sounded like she was beginning to uncover for herself.

"Well, yes—whether it's how to make the bed, being told it's not OK to hug his brother after their mom died, or telling me how to dress. I'm thirty-seven years old, I'm a successful executive, and all of a sudden, according to him, I don't know how to do anything right! The normal things I would do—just being me—aren't OK. I'm second-guessing myself, wondering whether maybe he's right and I've been doing things wrong all these years."

Albert resisted the urge to say "bull" to her, knowing that having been the vice president of several major companies, Eve had shown a healthy self-confidence until now. I'm getting more concerned by the minute, Albert thought to himself, because what she's saying fits a pattern I've read about. I don't want to alarm her, but I do have to ask a difficult question: "Do you think he would ever hit you?"

"I'm not sure anymore. He gets so angry all of a sudden—it's like I've stepped on a land mine—he just blows up. Or he'll go quiet, telling me, 'Just *think* about it,' when I ask what I've done wrong. When I try to explain myself or disagree with his interpretation, he gets even angrier. Sometimes I don't feel it's safe to stay in the house. I think I'm going crazy because he'll keep telling me that I didn't say what I said and he didn't say what he said. The other day, I was driving to work and felt like my body was covered in bruises. I thought to myself, "It's so strange. How come I feel beat up when I haven't been touched?"

By then Albert had heard enough. He asked her if she was open to some advice. He wanted her to take responsibility for making a decision to get help. He knew he wasn't an expert on verbally abusive relationships, but he'd read enough to know the warning signs. Albert told Eve, "Here's what I hear you saying about your relationship: You're confused and aren't sure what's causing these sudden outbursts. He gets angry over little things, and you don't think his reaction is reasonable. You are scared enough sometimes to think about leaving the house. You aren't sure of yourself anymore and feel like you can't do anything right. You spend a lot of time trying to avoid making him angry. He puts you down if you have a point of view that is different from his. And you feel as if you are being beaten by words that leave marks you can't see."

"Yes," Eve said slowly, her eyes widening as she began to get the picture of what was happening to her. "But he's really so great . . ." and she went on to defend her boyfriend, remembering the good times they'd treasured early on. "There's another wonderful side of him. Maybe this will all pass," she added, pointing out that they were in the normal adjustment phase of getting to know each other.

"I appreciate that you love him," Albert said softly, "and that you want to make this work. Most couples run into problems, and maybe that's all this is. But I want you to seriously consider that it could be something else. You'll need to decide for yourself, but I invite you to do some research on this. First, go to the Web, type in the words 'verbal abuse,' and learn about the symptoms. See if you recognize your relationship. Second, I urge you to talk to a therapist who specializes in this. See what a professional thinks. If you don't feel up to that yet, get a book on it and start there."

Then Albert asked if he could tell her a story from his childhood. She said sure, she could use a break from her story.

"It sounds like you are dealing with an emotional bully," Albert said slowly, with a faraway look in his eyes. "You're losing your confidence. You feel outmaneuvered and overpowered and are giving in to appease him and to avoid a fight. When you resist, you get verbally knocked down again and again. You try to explain yourself and get a verbal fusillade. You are developing ways of protecting yourself that are causing you to become increasingly invisible. That's what I did when I was tormented by a bully at school. The last thing you want to do with a bully is keep being nice and thinking it's all your fault or trying not to make the bully mad. It won't change the bully's behavior—such people have a need to dominate. You need to make choices about getting help."

It took Eve a couple of months to have the courage to get the information she needed, first from several Web sites. In the privacy of her own home, she faced the beginning of the truth. She was stunned that she hadn't been able to see it. Later she bought the book *The Verbally Abusive Relationship: How to Recognize It and How to Respond* by Patricia Evans and read stories of other women's experiences that sounded a lot like hers. She said it was comforting but also shocking. Several months went by before she and her boyfriend broke up. She needed that time to accept that she couldn't change things. Her friends had been telling her that the relationship didn't sound right; she didn't sound happy, and her spirit seemed crushed. Her mother was worried, too. Eve hadn't been able to act on their warnings because she kept thinking she and John would find a way out of their problems.

This story unfolded one night at the home of Eve's friends. After hearing it, one savvy former CEO blurted out a question: "Why didn't she just walk out the minute he started mistreating her and say, 'I'm not going to take it— I'm out of here!'?"

"Oh, I can tell you why," said another executive who had dealt with verbal abuse that had affected employees in his organization. "Verbal abuse is subtle. It sneaks up on you one incident at a time. The abused person— usually it's the woman—isn't always aware of what is happening. She thinks, If I just do this or do that or *don't* do that, he won't get angry anymore and it will be OK. But it's not. In the beginning, it can look like there is a victim and an abuser, but at some point the victim has to rise up from feeling like a helpless child and take adult action, which she can't do at first. Friends need to help her build up her strength to cross that bridge."

And that's what Eve did. One day, she let her boyfriend know that he had gone too far. He had told her she couldn't go to a work event that was important to her, and she had decided that she was going to go. That's when the relationship ended. She told me that the thing that helped her the most was friends who told her, "I'm so sorry that it didn't work out the way you'd hoped. I know you had big dreams and tried your best. We're ready to help you any way we can." None of them said, "I told you so." They understood that at the time, she couldn't get out because she kept thinking things would get better—they had been so beautiful in the beginning.

In the first few weeks of trying to recover, she started beating up on herself saying, "How could I have been so blind and stupid?" One friend told her, "Eve, you had to reach your own limits of not being willing to take it anymore. It will hurt for a while, and we'll be there to help you start a new life." One friend sensed that she might need to lighten up a bit, saying, "Honey, just think of it as one long blind date." That comment did help Eve have a much needed laugh at a painful time. What doesn't help is to say, "Look, he was a jerk. You deserve someone better." That kind of remark may be true, but it doesn't make the pain go away. Your friend may have had compassion for what made her lover a bully in the first place—many bullies have been bullied themselves. There is also that part of him that she loved and may still love no matter what he did to her.

The night I heard this story, what struck me was this: there were several men and women in the room, and each of us had had at least one experience with verbal abuse. Some grew up with verbally abusive parents. Others faced verbal abuse in the workplace. Several had verbally abusive lovers. One couple were volunteers at a battered women's shelter. One person had a neighbor who had sought refuge in his home from her verbally abusive husband. In the stories that were told, the abusers were both men and women. We were stunned to learn that this problem had affected all of us and how rarely it is discussed.

To be a better informed friend, neighbor, relative, or colleague, it's worth reading Patricia Evans's books, *The Verbally Abusive Relationship: How to Recognize It and How to Respond; Verbal Abuse Survivors Speak Out: On Relation-*

ship and Recovery; and *Controlling People: How to Recognize, Understand, and Deal with People Who Try to Control You.* I interviewed Patricia, asking her for guidelines to help us help someone recognize verbal abuse and recover from it. Her suggestions for recognizing verbally abusive relationships include the following:

- If someone tells you about an incident that bothers you, show dismay: "Oh, no, that's awful." Validate that what the person is experiencing is *not normal.*

- If people talk about feeling emotionally off balance or unsafe, make an offer they can take you up on anytime: "If you ever need a place to get away, you can stay with me."

- If they sound brainwashed into thinking that the problems are their fault, without sounding patronizing, gently contrast their situation with one that is normal: "Gee, most people talk things over when they don't agree. At least, that's the way it is in my family."

To help individuals recover after leaving a verbally abusive relationship, Patricia makes the following recommendations:

- Say things like "I've heard that it's very difficult to leave. It must have hurt to admit what was going on" or "I've never told you this, but I was once in an abusive relationship. If you want to know what helped, let's talk sometime."

- Don't say, "Get over it and move on." That invalidates the individuals' feelings, which is precisely what many verbally abused people experience when they are told by their abusers that they are "too sensitive" or that they "don't know what they are talking about." Instead, *try to restore their confidence* by asking their opinion about something that's important to you: "I value your thoughts. Tell me what you think about . . ."

- Don't ask, "Why did you stay?" There are lots of reasons people stay in these relationships. Confusion, hope, fear—but mostly because they suffered a slow destabilization of their sense of who they are and what's real. They need your help in hearing positive things they can believe. When they tell their hurtful stories, quietly let them know that *your* experience of who they are is different. "Your ex must have said a lot of things to make you doubt yourself. My experience of you is that you are decisive, capable, creative, thoughtful, . . ."

People who have endured both physical and verbal abuse will tell you that it can take longer to heal the scars carved by words than to mend broken skin and bones. That's why after someone has *left* a verbally abusive relationship, please don't make your first question, "Did he hit you?" As Eve explained, "Even if he didn't hit with his fists, he did hit with his words. And it hurts."

I Don't Want to Be a Burden

Supporting the widowed spouse

I've been left behind," she said almost to herself, as if she couldn't believe it had happened. "I don't belong here. I don't belong anywhere. He left without me. We've been together sixty years. How come I don't feel he is dead? I feel him right beside me. I can't even think of how to live without him because I still feel him here. Nobody understands how I feel!"

How do you facilitate a healing conversation between family members during the stressful transition time after a death? What if you don't know the family well? That's the situation I found myself in one afternoon when my client, Jason, asked me to come over to sit shiva* with his mother and his brother, Marvin. Jason had hinted that maybe I could help him and his brother stop going around in circles over what to do to help their newly widowed mother.

---

*Sitting shiva is a custom in the Jewish culture where family and friends visit the bereaved in their home to offer support during the first week after a death.

Sensing that Jason's mother didn't understand why others weren't feeling as lost as she was, I acknowledged her feelings by reassuring her. "Lots of people don't get to feel the kind of closeness you two had. It must feel strange for you that to everyone else, he seems gone, but to you he still is here."

"Yes, that's it exactly," she cried softly. "And I don't want to be a burden," she said to her sons. She looked like a scared little girl whose family was scattered around the country and whose friends had told her that they were too frail to safely look after her. Her fragility was one reason why her husband had finally agreed to move into an assisted living facility.

I sensed that she needed to get her bearings, to remember who she had been when the world wasn't feeling so out of control. I gently asked her, "Remember when your sons were kids and there were responsibilities you had as their parent? Things you had to do because it was the right thing to do?"

"Well, yes," she said slowly.

"Now is like that time, only they have responsibilities for you," I explained. "You aren't a burden, but you *are* a responsibility. That's why they are worried, because they won't feel as if they've done their job until they help you figure out the best next step."

"I need a week, a week to get my feet back on the ground," she said, her voice growing stronger. "And tell them, please tell them not to get rid of my things or make decisions without asking me first. I'm not dead yet, and there are things I still care about. Like my radio. They got rid of my radio without asking me."

"Mom," Jason said with hurt frustration, "the guys were there with the truck. We had to get everything moved."

"Yes, but you didn't ask me. I knew how to work that radio. It tuned in all my favorite stations and played good music."

"Mom, we'll get you another one," he said. "I just didn't think when we were moving you. It was more a matter of taking care of everything at once."

"I appreciate that, son, but that's not the point. That radio was just fine, and I knew how to work it," she said firmly. "In the future, I want you to ask me about my things. Don't assume, please."

It can feel awkward to be translating for others. It's important to remember to keep rephrasing what each person is saying—not to take sides but to help them hear one another. "It sounds like you are trying to tell your sons that when everything changes at once—where you live, that you are alone, that you aren't caring for someone around the clock anymore—little things, like a favorite radio, make all the difference. You're trying to help them appreciate that when things disappear, you feel disoriented, and you hang on to anything that is familiar. Anything. So even if you know you shouldn't drive or shouldn't live alone on the second floor because you can't climb the stairs, you hold on to what's familiar because everything seems to be changing."

"Yes," she said firmly, "and I'm afraid of something else. I'll look stupid to all the other people in the assisted living place because I don't know how to do things on my own—like go to the bank or pay the bills."

"That's ridiculous," Marvin said under his breath. "They've shown her how to do these things at the bank. They even balance her statements. What's she so worked up about?"

I told them what I'd learned a few weeks ago from some bank executives. Their elderly customers had helped them realize that they considered their trip to the bank an important occasion to talk and to have a sympathetic ear. Today some of the banks are teaching their tellers how to take the time and interest in these customers, rather than worrying that they were taking too much time and holding up the line. It took these banks a while to realize that they had to change their priorities from serving people quickly to actually connecting with the person on the other side of the counter in a way that had meaning, not just efficiency.

"What's she afraid of?" asked her elder son when his mother stepped out of the room for a few minutes. "We'll take care of her."

"Well," I explained, "it sounds like she's afraid something might happen to you and to your financial stability. Then where would she be?"

"I never thought of it that way," Marvin said softly. "It never occurred to me that she would be worried about money."

It can be frustrating, as Jason and Marvin found with their mother, to try to help a loved who is going through a transition from one way of life to another. It's hard for us to step into someone else's shoes, especially when we don't think we'd be having the problems she is having. This is one way an outsider can help provide perspective for a family. Sometimes it's easier to hear what someone you aren't related to is trying to say because you aren't tied to an umbilical cord of hopes, hurts, and needs.

When, like Jason, we hear ourselves saying to someone who needs our comfort, "I don't understand," that's a clue for us to pause and ask, "What am I missing here?" Taking the time to pause allows us to stop judging, stop reacting, and get curious. It allows us to tap into compassion at the very moment when, if we didn't pause, we might find ourselves saying or doing something that is misunderstood or that we'd regret. When people, like Jason's mother, let you know that you've done something that hurt their feelings, you may need to apologize and ask them to tell you what works and what doesn't as you learn along the way. Even when we think we know exactly what they need, it may not be at all what they want.

Splinters, Mice, and Little Things
Learning to live alone

Whether you are living alone by choice or by circumstance, there are times when you'd like friends to understand that it's not the big things that can get you down. That's what I learned one night when I tried to get a splinter out of my hand. I'm right-handed. The splinter was in my right hand. Ever try to use your other hand to do something that takes coordination? Not easy. Not easy at all. Add to that the realization that you've always had someone else around to take the darn things out.

That's when it hit me about living alone. It was just a little thing, this splinter. But in that one moment, late that night, in the little house I'd bought and where I was living by myself for the very first time, I realized what it meant to live alone. It's not the big challenges—negotiating a mortgage loan or dealing with blizzards, hurricanes, and floods. Somehow those situations didn't get to me. Those are instances when people expect you to turn to others for help. But at ten o'clock at night, you don't call up the one neighbor who you "kind of" know to ask for help with something as small as digging a splinter out of your hand. You think to yourself, Hey, it's no big deal, but in that moment I had this stupid, little-kid-like feeling of being alone and wanting someone with a caring touch to take care of a silly little hurt.

Another moment like this came when the floor moved. It was just a flash. I wasn't sure what I'd seen at first. Decided to ignore it. Until I saw it again later that night. Why do these things always happen at night? Again, the floor moved. Or so it seemed. Then I knew what it was. Little flicker of a tail. Mouse in the house. Gads, how come I never learned how to set the Have-a-Heart trap?

The next day, I went up to see the neighbor I couldn't bother about the splinter. Having a mouse in the house qualified for the "you can ask for help" list. Her husband spent about an hour (battling with arthritis and a touchy mousetrap) helping me figure out how to delicately set the hairpin trigger for the bait.

It's the little things that seem to add up over time so that suddenly a little thing feels like you can't take it anymore. It's helpful to know this because when a friend of yours starts living alone and little things start to seem bothersome, please remember that it's not just that one particular incident that's cratering your friend's life, it's the realization that no matter how big or small the problem is, when you live alone, you must deal with the fact that there is no one else to handle it. Sure, sometimes there is a freedom in that, because no one can foul up not paying the bills or fix something incorrectly or not ever fix it. However, the next little thing that goes wrong is one more reminder that there is no one but you to decide what to do. At that moment, if this happens to people you know, try to imagine what it would be like. Please don't say something like "It's just a little thing." They already know that. Let them tell you how it is for them on the good and bad days of coping with life on their own.

There are other ways you can be supportive to people who are living alone.

- Don't assume that they want company, but do offer to visit—they may miss having someone to cook for or eat with, or perhaps they'd like you to join them on a walk.

- Offer to spend a morning, afternoon, or evening with them—perhaps take in a movie, take a drive, or visit a favorite spot they'd rather not go to alone.

- If you are handy, ask if there's anything you can to do help around the house or apartment—whether it's repairs or something that takes two sets of hands.

- Offer to introduce them to anyone you might know in their area who could become a resource or even a friend.

- Invite them to visit you and even to stay overnight for a few days if they live far away. This can be especially helpful during those awkward times when they might find it uncomfortable to be alone, such as on their birthday, a particular holiday, or during the summer when it seems that so many others have family plans.

Broken Hearts and Burnt Offerings

When a gift offers a reservoir of care

A PACKAGE ARRIVED. IT WASN'T MY BIRTHDAY, AND I KNEW I HADN'T ORDERED anything from a catalogue. Who was sending me something? Unwrapping the package, I found myself holding a most extraordinary heart, about the size of my palm. It was made of jagged pottery fragments—different-colored earth-tone pieces mysteriously held together by an invisible force. The heart was a gift sent by a friend who sensed that in the aftermath of my divorce, this first Valentine's Day might be a reminder of unfinished dreams.

Sometimes we can go beyond a phone call or a visit to send someone something that speaks to us in its own way—whether it is a token to let a friend know you are thinking of him or her, something of yours that has special meaning, or an item that may, like this heart, symbolize more than your words could say. The gift took on even more meaning when I read the artist's story of how he makes the hearts. He makes these one-of-a-kind hearts by creating a beautiful pottery work, smashing it to bits, and then fitting the different-colored pieces together to make a new whole.

As the years passed, Valentine's Day became easier to bear, and yet this gift took on new meaning each time I faced a difficult situation. It was like a reservoir of care that I could return to when I needed a lift, some encouragement that what felt torn or rent would eventually mend. Gifts from the heart keep on giving long after someone's pain fades.

The gift was accompanied by a piece of writing that was as remarkable as the handcrafted heart. I reprint it here with permission from the gentle artist and author, Richard Bohn.

BURNT OFFERINGS

These hearts of mine, these thin clay envelopes enclosing the often tedious moments of both our becoming, I hurl, with confident hubris, into the future, only to dodge their flaming fall, shattering at my feet.

After resurrection I discover them full of memories, seeping slowly from fine fissures, drop by drop, filling my heart.

If you let your fingers trace the sharp edge of these jagged shards, be mindful, for you teeter near a crevasse, whose abysmal floor is littered with broken vows, failed dreams, and the white brittle bones of hope. Not only yours, but your mother's, and father's, grandparent's, great grandparent's and beyond. Look deep into this chasm and watch it fill with the debris of human experience.

Why do these tender, bruised fragments, which fit together so very beautifully into ancient forms, complete in their brokenness, remembering their wholeness, and beckoning quietly to us, serve as inspiration to follow?

These hearts of mine have experienced pain, but it is my wish that whosoever sees them, touches them, remembers them, or hears of them, is inspired by hope. That in our breaking lies our wisdom. Our own becoming, beautiful, after our healing.

What Is Enough?

Retirement as a way of life

I CAN'T TELL YOU HOW MANY PEOPLE JOKINGLY ASKED ME, 'SO HOW'S YOUR golf game, Byrd?' I don't even play golf! I know that many people don't know what to say to you after you retire. It's awkward for them, so they make quips or genuinely don't know what you're doing with your time. What I appreciated was when someone would ask me, 'So what are you doing now that you didn't have time to do before you retired?' Or 'What are you doing in retirement that you find enjoyable?'"

Byrd's story, which is also his wife Alice's story, gives us clues about what's going on behind the scenes before, during, and after the last goodbyes at the office are said. How can we appreciate the complexity of this transition? What do we say to someone who is retiring or to someone who responds to our "What do you do for a living?" question with the blunt answer, "Well, I'm retired."

"I think people don't know what to say to us because they're scared," Byrd's wife Alice said. "They're scared about whether they're going to be OK when they retire. I didn't retire from my work until a few years after Byrd left his job. However, when I was thinking about how I wanted to view myself in retirement, one thing was very important to me: I didn't want retirement to change the way that I engaged with the world or the world engaged with me. I didn't want people to think that just because I retired from my national and local community service positions, I was going to go fallow. It's also scary because you don't know whether you will have enough of what you think you'll need to take care of yourself and to enjoy what's important to you. Twenty years before Byrd retired, we started having serious conversations to help us define what 'enough' was for us."

"What helped you decide what was enough?" I asked.

Alice replied, "Our definition of 'enough' wasn't based on comparing ourselves to others. We wanted to be able to take one or two trips a year doing things we enjoyed. We wanted to be able to visit our kids. We didn't want to always buy the cheapest things, but we also wanted to have enough left that we could give money away—whether it was to friends, to family, or to charity. We were fortunate that we had a pension plan from Byrd's company and that our health insurance was taken care of, too. We know that a lot of people don't have that security, and we were grateful to have both covered."

"What was the hardest thing about the first year in retirement?" I asked.

"Oh, that's easy," Alice chuckled. "Byrd had to adjust to managing his own schedule and doing ordinary things like troubleshooting the computer. For most of his career, his staff had booked him for ten to twelve hours a day, and suddenly he was the one booking himself and taking care of 'office' challenges that his staff had handled. Meanwhile, I had to get used to having him in the house all day. I'd worked from home and wasn't used to being inter-rupted, and suddenly he'd be there, wanting to talk. It took a while for both of us to stop stepping on each other's toes and to make room for him to have a space of his own."

For Byrd, the biggest change, though, wasn't dealing with the invasion of physical space—it was adjusting to making room for *emotional* space.

> Not having my life run by a tight schedule gives me room to make more choices. Recently, when I traveled for work, I took the time to spend with friends and with my son and spent a day at the museum seeing an exhibit of one of my favorite artists. Before I was retired, I would have flown in to the city, gotten the job done, and told myself that I'll get back some other time to see people and to see the exhibit. Of course, that wouldn't happen.

> The most obvious difference about being retired is in the way Alice and I spend time together. It's richer. Richer because I can lis-ten to Alice talk about taking a walk in the woods and appreciate her excitement about discovering which little wildflowers bloomed that day. Before I retired, I would have thought, Look, I don't have time to sit here and chat about the flowers—I barely have time to sit here! Can't we talk about something more important? Today, I relax and enjoy her joy. There are other times when she'll be telling me something and instead of reacting the way I used to react—think-ing, OK, how can I fix this?—now I realize that all she wants from me is to listen. Before, it felt like she was taking too long to get to the point. Today, I realize it's not about her getting to any point. The only point is to let her share whatever she wants to share. If she needs me to fix anything, she'll ask.

Byrd and Alice were eight years into retirement and still adjusting to its new rhythms. Once Byrd had ended his thirty-one years at IBM, it brought everything in their relationship to a head. They'd had to talk to a relationship therapist and work on their communication skills. It was rough for a while, prompting Alice to give this advice to those going through retirement and those of us who want to support them: "You need friends to help with the transition into retirement. Whether these are new friends or lifelong friends— the key to enjoying retirement is having them around you. You need to talk about the changes you are going through, the questions you haven't answered, and the inevitable health challenges that crop up."

It can be frustrating to wonder how you are going to make it once you're retired. These observations from retirees can help us be more sensitive to their transitions:

- Please don't assume I'm just going to play golf and putter around all day. Just because I'm not earning a paycheck anymore doesn't mean I'm not contributing to society.

- Give me credit for still having a brain. I've simply stopped going to a regular job; nothing is wrong with my capacity to think, learn, teach, and even work if I want to work.

- Maybe I'm bitter about being forced out of a job I wasn't ready to leave.

- I'm adjusting to not having my old schedule. If I seem a bit scattered, don't think I've lost my mind; I've just not found my new focus yet.

What Happens When You Show Up for Class?

Lessons from an elder

WHAT DOES IT MEAN TO HAVE AN APPRECIATION FOR GETTING OLDER—TO remember that older people have a lot to teach us? How do we let them know they matter, especially when they don't think they do? The fact that they can't always move and think as quickly as they used to teaches us how to value life taken at a more deliberate pace—one step, one word, or in the case of Mary, one stroke at a time.

Mary's head was bent over the curve of her worn cane as she sat on the bench waiting for her Aquacize class to begin. A faint smell of chlorine floated in the air. Janine walked to the end of the corridor where she sat and said, "Looks like it's just us today."

"Oh, no," said Mary with quiet confidence. "The others will be along soon."

She looked at Janine with eyes that wondered what Janine was doing in this class. "Do you have arthritis?" she asked, thinking that Janine was much too young to be here.

"No," Janine explained. "But I have a hard-to-treat condition, and my therapists hope that swimming will build up my strength."

"Oh," Mary murmured, looking down at her swollen knee. "I tore my knee some fifty years ago skiing; that's how I got my arthritis. I can't stand, kneel, or walk. This is the only thing I can do, this class. It's not easy, having a knee that won't bend. You should have seen what it was like back in the days when you had to kneel down to light the old gas stoves. I didn't want my children to see me—how hard it was to do something so simple as to light the stove. You learn to live with it, though."

Just at that moment, the other ladies showed up. Laughing and ambling along with their canes, which promptly got hung up along side their multi-colored towels. In a few minutes, they were silently slipping down the special stairs into the ninety-degree pool. Free to float. Free of the weight of their pain.

Wearing her neon purple suit, the teacher bounced into the pool. Suddenly they were doing "the routine" to music from the '40s. There was laughter and jokes. This was a lighthearted family troupe moving in circles, flexing fingers, sliding across the shallow end of the YWCA pool, moving like slightly tipsy people through the water.

Janine had come to the class because therapists told her that Aquacize was her last hope. No one really seemed to know how to strengthen her body, which was plagued with injuries. She'd tried everything. Today was it. She was supposed to find out if the water exercises would help.

Janine explained, "It wasn't easy for me to get in that pool with what could be my future staring me in the face. The stoic lady I'd met in the locker room had torn her knee skiing when she was in her thirties. I tore my knee when I was in my thirties, I told her, thinking it was no coincidence that she and I were sharing stories.

"As we walked through the pool, flapping our arms, kicking our legs, it felt like what we were doing wasn't going to help build the muscles I needed," Janine explained. "It was too easy. However, instead of getting out of the pool or resigning myself to being stuck there, I decided that I was there for a reason other than a cure, so I might as well really show up and pay attention to what else was going on in the class."

It was just about that moment when Mary turned to Janine in the pool. They had wound up right next to each other at the end of the last exercise round. Mary quietly observed, "I'm not good at anything." She'd been staying in the very shallow end—being the oldest (eighty-seven years) and the shortest (four foot ten) of the group—and not wanting to get into water over her head. She suddenly looked sad and alone.

Janine turned to Mary and said, "Well, you do have a wonderful laugh." And she did. That made Mary laugh—the kind of laugh that crinkles up a face in a way that lights the space around it. Then as Janine was about to water-walk away with the '40s music swishing her along, she turned again to Mary and said, "I'll bet you have grandchildren."

"Great-great-grandchildren!" Mary said proudly.

"You see, then," Janine said, "it doesn't sound like you aren't good for anything at all." Mary laughed again and floated off in her own world.

Later that afternoon, Janine talked to her friend Rick. "You know, Rick, I think the reason I was in that class today wasn't about getting a cure. I think it was to meet Mary. I was there to learn a lesson from her: that if you just show up and don't get too hung up on what you thought was going to happen, you get exactly what you need."

As it turned out, the real teacher wasn't the bouncy lady in the sleek-fitting purple passion suit. It was eighty-seven-year-old Mary, in her blue-and-green flowered skirt suit, who doesn't have to really know how to do anything other than to be herself—a great-great-grandmother with a sore knee and a laugh that can fill a ladies' locker room with light.

The gift of healing that Jeanine offered a total stranger was to shift from being on automatic pilot. When it looked like she wouldn't get what she'd hoped for in the class, she paused to get in touch with her own feelings of hopelessness, allowing her to compassionately relate, minutes later, to a fellow human being who was also feeling a bit useless that day.

I Know *Her* Name
> *Living with Alzheimer's*

The most helpful things we learned about taking care of my mother were to realize that she isn't who she was, to stop trying to get her to 'remember when . . . ,' and to tell her stories about the past as if she were hearing them for the first time. The hardest thing I've learned is that what's important to Momma isn't what she remembers—she can't remember—but what she experiences with me right here and now, one minute at a time."

Each week, it seems that a friend or a colleague learns that their mother, father, husband, or wife has Alzheimer's. How can we possibly comfort someone who in the days, weeks, and years ahead will be coping with the gradual but disorienting changes in the person they love?

For Alicia, her mother's Alzheimer's was most noticeable after Alicia's dad died. That's when it began to be more obvious that her mother could not take care of herself.

"I'll never forget that day. We'd just come from visiting my dad at the hospital. He had been diagnosed with cancer and had become very ill. As soon as we got home, Momma insisted that we needed to go right back to visit Dad. It was as if we had not even been there. When I told her we couldn't go back there right now, she became agitated and grabbed my arm so forcefully that it left a bruise. Alarmed, I told her, "Momma, you've got to stop this. I'm going to call the doctor." She flew out the kitchen, slamming the door behind her so hard it shattered the mirror on the wall in the next room. At that moment, when she became furious with me for not taking her to see my dad, I realized that I'd become a frightened child again. I didn't want my mother mad at me."

"So what do you do," I asked her, "when your parent goes into a rage over something that doesn't make sense to you?"

"You stop and realize that you can't keep acting like that person's child. You take on the role of seeing the person—your mother, in my case—as someone unrelated to you, just as you would if you were a caregiver. It's not that you don't love her. It's that you have to detach yourself from being hooked by her irrational and often hurtful or confusing behavior. You have to step out of the behavior patterns you developed over decades. You also have to stop thinking that you can change her behavior."

Families with Alzheimer's eventually have to navigate their way through wrenching decisions about home care and assisted living. But, Alicia said, her family's most difficult decision wasn't about placing her mother in long-term care, which they did finally do.

"The most difficult decision you have to make is about how to patiently and lovingly respond, moment to moment, to the person you love—someone who may be angry, frustrated, content, confused, or unintelligible—as if she were a totally different person from the one you thought you knew. The person she was isn't there anymore. There is a whole other person lost inside trying to find her way. Especially in the later stages of Alzheimer's, there is a constant need for the patient to be oriented to the surrounding world. For example, one day, my mother tried to get out of the car. But she could no longer understand the concept of turning around. We kept trying to explain to her what she needed to do. But she had no way to communicate to us that she didn't know what she didn't know."

"Is there something that you have learned that has changed the way you would like people to think about Alzheimer's?" I asked.

❱ It took us a long time to stop trying to get Momma to remember her past and to remember who we were. Expecting someone with Alzheimer's to remember her life stories is like expecting someone who is paralyzed to walk. It helped when we stopped asking her, "Do you remember . . . ?" and started retelling old stories by saying something like, "Remember when we had that special Fourth of July celebration and we . . . ?" When we retold the stories as if for the first time, it became a form of entertainment to her, and we let go of needing her to remember or to do anything other than be with us then and there.

As the Alzheimer's progressed, Momma taught me something else. She totally redefined my concept of friendship. To my astonishment, she made friends with a woman in the nursing home who was twenty years her senior. They couldn't remember each other's names or each other's stories, but it didn't seem to matter. I couldn't imagine a friendship on those terms, and yet Momma showed me it was not only possible but even joyful.

The truth is that Momma is doing better with her illness than we are. She isn't dying of anything—she is living with Alzheimer's. And though some in my family have said, and I used to agree with them, that they thought she would be better off if she passed away, I no longer agree with that sentiment. Now that she is in the later stages of Alzheimer's, on most days, Momma is content. It's not for me to judge that she isn't entitled to be the way she is, even if that means she is a totally different person from the mother I knew. The pain is ours, not hers.

Alicia talked about what friends or colleagues could do or say to support someone who is caring for a loved one with Alzheimer's:

- We appreciate it if you quietly listen to us talk about our worries about the future and what will happen.
- It's a good idea to have someone who didn't know our loved one well, or at all, come along to visit. We won't be thinking of their past—just who they are now.
- It's OK to ask how our loved one is doing. Just remember that things aren't going to get better, so don't expect a glowing report.

Each family's experience with Alzheimer's is different. In some families, there are painful fights and even court proceedings over what kind of care to provide a parent. It's hard to know how to support someone who may want you to take sides. In another case, a friend whose mother had Alzheimer's admitted, months after his mother died, that when she was still alive, he wished he'd been able to talk to friends about how angry and helpless he felt each time he visited his mom. Seeing his bitter and angry mother, as he put it, "wither away in a living purgatory," he needed to be able to say to someone who wouldn't think he was an uncaring son, "When is this all going to end?"

Or a wife wishes she could turn to her best friend to ask his advice, only to remember that he's the one with Alzheimer's. What can you say when she tells you that she wishes he were "there" to help her decide what to do? In these cases, there is nothing we can do to restore their loved one's memory or personality. Over and over again, friends and family will say, "Just let me talk about my experiences—whether they are frustrating, terrifying, or humbling. And please don't ask me whether she knows my name. Try to remember that I know hers."

The Long Goodbye
When death takes its time

I KEPT THINKING AS I SAT NEXT TO MY DAD'S BED, "HE DOESN'T HAVE MUCH time left—I should be having meaningful conversations with him." The more I tried to think of something important to say or do, the farther away I felt from my father. It took a while for me to let go of myself and just be with him without an agenda."

Martina's father had been diagnosed with inoperable but treatable lymphoma. She was living in another state and was commuting back and forth to visit him. The commuting was taking a toll on her life partner, her business, and her health. She felt torn in many directions. Her story helps us appreciate the hidden opportunities for healing that some family members seize during the time when a person's life is ending. We're also reminded that some family members aren't up to the task of sorting through their unfinished business with the person who is dying, leaving a wake that outlasts the funeral.

At first there was a lot to do when Dad was hospitalized. We mobilized to get as much medical information as possible. I started commuting back and forth. My brothers and their wives took turns being with Mom at the hospital and bonding with each other while cleaning out their house. Then reality set in. This could go on indefinitely.

I had to ask myself: OK, how else could you set your life up to make this work? I spoke to my partner, Adrienne, who said she would support my relocating back home and look after our house for as long as it took. Next, I had to talk to my clients. As a consultant, I knew that they could just as easily work with someone else, rather than put up with the inconvenience of my commuting or being unavailable—emotionally or physically. I was afraid that while my father was dying, my business might die too.

My clients stunned me with their support. "Do what you need to do," they said. "We understand you need to be there with him. We'll be here when you get back." Some even gave me business leads in the state where my Dad lived.

Martina's friends supported her during this long goodbye by letting her go. They checked in with her to see how she and her dad were doing, but they didn't expect her to reciprocate as if nothing had happened. Some helped her decorate her new place, and one sent a "care package" of vitamins, books, and comforting items to her new apartment. Her friends made sure she knew that she still mattered to them.

After I relocated, I was faced with how to spend time with Dad. He'd been a pretty private person, and at first I felt awkward with him. I was the only daughter in a family of sons, and we hadn't hung out much together. In time, I learned that all he wanted was my company. To have me sit with him during his X-rays, to take him for a drive, to go out for breakfast—to let go of my agenda of having meaningful conversations about important topics. I learned to stop thinking about the past or the future and to focus on what was going on for him at that moment. For example, if he was in a lot of pain, he felt awful and *I* felt awful and there would often be nothing I could do. But instead of fussing or feeling guilty, I was able to be silent with him and to feel him feeling his pain without my trying to push it away.

"How did the rest of your family cope with this long goodbye?" I asked Martina.

My older brother did OK, but the younger one had a difficult time. When he got sick, my father asked my younger brother to take over the business. It was thriving at the time. But in almost no time, the practice began to fail. After Dad died, my brother decided he couldn't keep the practice open, and he walked away, leaving us with a messy situation. He and Dad had had many talks about how to keep the business going, but my brother felt like he'd been a big disappointment to Dad his whole life.

The thing that caused a lot of problems was that my younger brother didn't help us close up the company. He just walked out. Near the end, Dad felt clueless as to how to help his youngest son deal with what had been a long-festering problem. Dad wasn't pleased with the way things were ending, and it made him sad. Years later, this unfinished business is still causing problems for our family.

As in Martina's case, there are family members who aren't able to resolve their upsets with a dying loved one. It would be easy to think of them as selfish or stubborn. After all, we think to ourselves, time was running out. Couldn't they set aside their hurts and make peace? However, what if we try to appreciate how much they might have wanted to find peace and for whatever reason were unable to? We can't know what it takes for one person to forgive another. For some people, to tell the truth about something they've kept secret, to say they are sorry, or to acknowledge that they never understood can take more than we may imagine.*

It's possible that in time, the family member who didn't get to tie things up before a death may want our help (or the help of trained professionals) in having that conversation months or even years later. There can still be a chance for healing through journaling, letter writing, psychodrama or other role-play therapy, counseling, or energetic healing. Or the person may not want anyone's help. If someone isn't ready to discuss forgiveness, we need to respect that decision.

"You've talked about things that were left unsaid," I noted. "Was there anything else that your family did that helped you get a sense of completion with your dad?"

Yes, I almost forgot to share this. We asked my dad if we could get everyone in the family together to tell him whatever we wanted to say to him. It was a ceremony of letting him know what he meant to us. He said yes, except for one condition: no one was to feel that

---

*In *Forgiveness Is a Choice,* Professor Robert Enright helps us understand the pain and promise of making a decision about whether we are ready to forgive ourselves or someone else.

he or she *had* to say something. We could all just be in the room. We gathered in a circle, and soon we were telling him what we wanted to say.

Everyone spoke easily until it was the turn of one of my dad's nephews. He couldn't say anything. Looking gently at the young man, my father chimed in, "It's OK. I know how you feel about me," and smiled.

Thinking that the family had come together in the final days of her father's life, I asked Martina when the ceremony took place. "Oh, nine months before he died," she answered. "We didn't know how much time we had, and we told him we didn't want to wait until he was too ill to be able to understand what we were saying or until it was too late."

Martina's father gave his family a gift of healing by allowing them to share their feelings with him. However, it's important to remember that not everyone will let us say goodbye. There are some people who won't even allow us to mention that they are dying, let alone permit us to tell them what they mean to us. While it is their right to keep that distance, if we are robbed of that chance to tell them how we feel, it can take longer for us to be at peace with their death. Years later, we may need our friends to help us find another way.

He Knows He's About to Die

🖎 *Visiting a friend in a hospice*

WHEN A FRIEND IS APPROACHING THE FINAL DAYS OF LIFE—WHETHER AT home, in a hospital, or a hospice facility—it's often awkward for a visitor to know what to say. How do we know what would really comfort someone who is dying? What would support the family who may be keeping a round-the-clock vigil? We're not family—should we even visit? One couple's story offers a window not just into the world of hospice care but also into how we can be ourselves with someone who is very near death.

After fighting Langdon's cancer for several years, the time came when he and his wife, Annabelle, decided that he should enter a hospice care facility. Langdon was a large man who required a strong team to bathe him and change his bedding. Langdon and Annabelle's studio apartment in Manhattan was too small to accommodate a private nurse or home care.

The decision to go to a hospice was gut-wrenching, as the two knew that this was foreshadowing the end and that they would never share their loving bed together again. However, hospice care brings great comfort. It means that the patient will have the round-the-clock attention of professionals, many of whom are extraordinarily compassionate and are trained in the best ways to minimize pain. The hospice staff also attend to psychological and spiritual needs as well as provide the primary caregiver some time at home for reflection, tears, and gathering strength for the impending loss.

Annabelle set about creating as homey an environment as possible in Langdon's hospice room. He had been ravaged by the disease, become pathetically gaunt, and seemed to age overnight. That's why she made sure the room was sprinkled with photographs of him in his prime—photos with his family and a dashing photo of him in his British Commando uniform. His wife felt that the pictures reminded the nursing staff of what a strong, virile gentleman he once was, and this helped generate and enhance respect and fondness toward him.

Annabelle also composed a list of suggestions to help visitors feel less awkward during their visits. Here is how it read:

> Langdon knows he is dying. I know this might be awkward for some of you, so in my gratitude for your being here, here is a list that might help you. Please accept it in the spirit it is intended—as a way to comfort and to bring sweet peace to Langdon.
>
> - Try to get beyond the shock of his appearance. I know it is sad and grim, but it is our wonderful Langdon inside this cancer-ravaged body.
>
> - Langdon is a gentleman with great dignity. If for some reason his blankets are askew in an immodest way, straighten them up for him, please.

- Langdon is a very tactile person. Feel free to hold his hand or stroke his arm. It is a wonderful way to connect.

- Talk to him about something besides his sickness—politics, the latest news, an anecdote from your friendship, some juicy gossip. And a good joke is always welcomed.

- Tell him what he means to you. Do not fear tears—they are natural—and words of friendship and love are the best ingredients in a farewell.

- Ask him if there are any phone calls you can make for him.

- There are times when Langdon won't seem totally lucid because of the pain medication, but he is very much aware of your presence and loves to just feel your being with him. This is often when handholding is a good gesture.

- If you sense that he needs more pain medication or if he tells you he needs it, please contact his nurse immediately.

- I will be here part of every day, but if you notice something that doesn't sit right with you regarding his comfort or his care, please call me to report it. This will be very helpful. Leave any messages on our tape.

- Please sign our visitors' poster and write a message if you find Langdon asleep.

Friends, thank you for coming to be with Langdon. Have a good visit.

Love, Annabelle

"What else do you think people need to know that could help support the family of someone who is dying in a hospice facility?" I asked.

> I always felt guilty for the times I could not be there sitting with him day and night. And yet there were times when I wanted to escape and take a walk, be back in our home, or go out and have a quiet meal away from the hospice environment. I also needed to have a good restorative cry and wanted to share things with my children about Langdon's condition.
>
> What took some of the burden of guilt from me was having a friend call and ask if he or she could fill in for me at the hospice, even give me a full day off. These offers were like manna from heaven, as I knew Langdon would understand my taking a break and would enjoy a new face to share a long visit with him. I made sure it was someone whom Langdon enjoyed. I should add that there were some people, well-meaning, whom he didn't want to visit him, and I would have to politely fend them off by saying, "Not a good day, I'm afraid, but thank you for the show of caring."

Something else friends might want to know is that telephone calls from people inquiring about the dying person's condition are not always welcome. Annabelle explained that she was exhausted, depressed, and frightened—lost in her own misery. "I just didn't have the energy to recite the mantra of my husband's grim deterioration to people who were perhaps phoning out of a sense of obligation. Often I fielded calls by letting the machine answer them. Later, I would respond to the meaningful ones. It's not easy to maintain perfect manners when your heart is breaking. Don't beat yourself up about this."

We were about to end our conversation when Annabelle looked out into the winter sky and said, "The most loving act you can do for one you love who is about to die is to listen to his thoughts. Be generous in sharing him with others who love him as much as you do. Arrange a private visit with a minister. Help him facilitate final amends that he expresses a desire to make. Listen to his fears and try to soothe them. Tell him how much you are going to miss him. Cry together. But most of all, share, if you can, an understanding that we all die and it is part of the continuum of life in which all suffering ends and love is eternal."

Anniversaries of Loss

Special dates to remember

Year after year, anniversaries can be a bittersweet time when we revisit memories and sometimes see the lives of the ones we have loved and lost in a new light. We need friends and colleagues to appreciate that the passing of time may actually deepen our loss.

When was the last time you wrote a thank-you note to your mom or dad? That's what I did today while I took a walk. My dad's been gone for thirteen years, but there were still some things I needed to tell him. I was thinking of him because today would have been his eightieth birthday. Like many people who face the anniversary of a loved one's death, I was wondering how to acknowledge the role he'd had in my life.

I thanked him for giving me my love of words. For teaching me there's value in doing things the "hard" way. Appreciating his gentle, soft Irish charm, the way he always seemed to have a genuine greeting for people no matter what their station in life. He left them feeling touched by his dancing blue eyes or his laugh.

During the course of this day of appreciating Dad's gifts to me, a client called to cancel a session. He explained that his family had just decided to go out to visit the grave of his mother, who had passed away six years ago that day. I left him a message saying that ironically, I, too, was honoring the love of a parent who had died. Maybe remembering was in the air.

For some people, it's not unusual for an anniversary to be a time of mixed emotions. We may still have unfinished business with the one we loved. In my case, this thank-you note didn't come easily. It had taken me years to come to terms with the fact that Dad disappeared without a word—for six years—after my mother left him in a bitter divorce. I'd seen him in the years that followed his reappearance, but it was never the same. Being able to accept him for who he was, not who he wasn't, had taken time.

No wonder we often don't know what to say when someone mentions the anniversary of the death, or the birthday, of someone who has died. Sometimes we say we're sorry, change the subject, or withdraw in awkward silence. Yet often people would like to share a story about the person they are remembering. Or they may want to be left alone with their private thoughts but not have you drop into an uncomfortable silence when they tell you it's an anniversary day.

You can support employees or coworkers by remembering these anniversary dates. You don't have to say anything—just be aware that this could be a sensitive time for them. One executive told colleagues that he had to pull off the road on the way to work one morning when it hit him that this was the day, one year ago, that he'd last seen his mom alive. When he got to work, he was overwhelmed with how much he missed her. He had never dreamed that he would feel this way. He also didn't expect to wind up sitting in his office in tears. He said that what helped him get through the day was his deciding to tell his staff that it was the first anniversary of his mother's passing and he was having a hard time "keeping it together." They appreciated that he told them what was going on and that he didn't pretend that his personal life could be left outside the office door. And after all, when you come right down to it, there really is no such thing as an "impersonal" life. It's all personal, isn't it?

If you have friends or family members who have lost someone, there is something you can do that may support them in the months and years after the death. Mark on your calendar the anniversary of the death or, if you know it, the birth date of the one who died. You can send a card or give a call around that time to acknowledge this special day of loss. There are other occasions when this sense of loss may be heightened: Mother's Day, Father's Day, holidays, a birthday, the graduation of a child from college, a wedding.

One last thought comes from Liz, who offers this guidance for all who find themselves at a loss for words when trying to comfort someone who has lost a parent.

> ❧ There are people who have lost their parents, and then there is the rest of the world. In my experience, if you haven't yet lost a parent, you live in a lot of fear of that day. You can't imagine it. When you lose a parent, for a while, the only people you feel can understand you are the ones who have lost parents, too. Often only they can appreciate some of the strange things we do, or what we laugh at, when we talk about our parents after they have died. When my dad died, it was hard for most people to appreciate why we had

placed a blanket over my dad's feet in the casket. Every night, when my parents went to bed, I would hear through the door, "Milton, Milton, move over, your feet are cold." Mom placed a lap blanket over his feet so that from that day forward, his feet would never be cold again. These are the memories we relive on anniversaries!

Reflection

 # Being with Their Silence— *and* Yours

There's another way to create a healing frequency: Give the gift of silence or caring attention. Appreciate that sometimes your colleagues, friends, or relatives may be in a place where they don't want to talk. They just want a caring presence, and they don't want you to feel uncomfortable with their silence or with yours. They don't have the energy to worry about making you feel comfortable.

For some people, it's easy to be comfortable with silence. For others, like me, it has taken a while to learn how to sit there and just be with someone, sending healing thoughts or silently appreciating being together.

It can help to gently ask if the person would like some quiet time— perhaps just being with you at that moment or sitting or walking outside somewhere or quietly holding hands. You can ask if she would like to take a break from talking to listen to some favorite music while both of you go off into your own thoughts yet share the same space. Or you can ask if he would like to rest for a while but know that you are somewhere close by—in another room reading, writing, cooking, cleaning up, or taking a little quiet time for yourself, too.

These are all ways you can provide comfort in the silence that can gently surround but not overwhelm you and the one you want to support. All it takes is a little practice, and perhaps, from time to time, learning how to be with yourself, as my teacher Jan Smith says, "in the silence that gives life meaning."* It is often only in the silent spaces between the words that we can truly hear the unspoken heart.

- If you would like to become more comfortable spending time with someone when talking isn't what's needed, think about what makes it difficult for you to be in silence. Does it feel meaningless to you, as if you're not doing anything to help? Or maybe it feels as if you will lose your composure—start crying, give in to anger, despair, sadness—if the talking stops and the feelings start coming up?

- Consider first learning how to spend time in reflection by yourself—whether learning to calm your "talking mind" through meditation or just sitting quietly and appreciating one

*Stephen Levine's books *Healing into Life and Death* and *One Year to Live* and Jon Kabat-Zinn's *Wherever You Go, There You Are* are helpful guides to developing a capacity for silence and for being in the presence of another's pain.

or two people or circumstances in your life. You might then practice being in silence with others by occasionally choosing to let the talking stop and bridging the gap with nothing more than quietly holding the other person, offering a gentle touch, or silently appreciating being together.

CHAPTER FIVE

Lost Loves

Leo the Cat

🐾 *Putting a "four-footed angel" to sleep*

Many of us don't even call them pets. They're members of our family. However, not everyone sees it that way. That's why when a family pet dies, we often don't know what to say. One night, a spontaneous conversation emerged in e-mail among a group of friends. We never realized that it would teach us not just about our love of pets but also about our relatives.

Andrea wrote to share some sad news:

> 🐾 At 2:00 this morning, I had to have my cat, Leo, put to sleep. Leo was my fluffy love bug of a cat who came to us about 6 years ago. Someone had brought him into my vet's office more dead than alive. His feet were burned, he had only a tuft of fur at the end of his tail, and he weighed 3 lbs. I'll never forget seeing this creature rubbing his face on the cage, as if to say, "Please love me."

By Christmas, Leo had turned into a beautiful Norwegian forest cat. Love and affection were his trademark. He taught us how to let the world take care of itself. He would first sit in your lap (always asking first). Then he would look in your eyes as if to say, "Be here with me now, for this is the time that counts."

Last night, about midnight, I heard a howl. I ran downstairs to find my Leo paralyzed in his hindquarters and in pain. I rushed him to the emergency vet. We had known for some time Leo had a heart murmur. His heart had thrown out a blood clot that had stopped the flow of blood to his back legs. His lungs filled with fluid, and the pain was strong. At about 2:00 as I held him in my arms, he was put to sleep. Leo truly knew how to be with the ones he loved and to love the ones he was with. We will miss you, Leo, as one of God's fine creatures.

I wrote a message to Andrea, which also went out to the group. Here is an excerpt:

Thank you for telling us about the love that Leo brought into your life. That you were able to let yourself love and be loved by him, knowing of his fragile state, shows how willing you were to let love in and to give it freely.

When our nine-year-old miniature dachshund, Daphne, died suddenly of a rare blood disease, my husband screamed NOOOOOOO, crying that he had lost his best friend. Despite blood transfusions, the devoted vets were unable to save her.

Daphne had given us the kind of love that you read about but rarely experience in humans. She would jump for joy when we came home even if she'd been alone for ten hours while we were at work. She would curl up with us and be very, very quiet when we were upset—knowing, somehow, that all we needed was comfort. These were the expressions of unconditional love that we so yearn for from the humans in our lives. I think that is why, when a pet dies, we are bereft beyond words.

Many people don't realize that sometimes a way of life, a way of loving or being loved, dies with a pet. One friend had a family service for his sweet little dog, who was hit by a car. Today there are flowers at the pup's grave. To this day, six years later, we haven't been able to scatter Daphne's ashes. When my husband and I ended our marriage, he wanted to keep the porcelain urn with her ashes. We just can't seem to let her go.

One reason I wanted to write about supporting others through the loss of a pet is because even if you can't feel our pain, you can help by letting us know you care. There were some people where I worked at the time of Daphne's death who didn't know what the "big deal" was about the death of a dog. One guy said, "Well you can go get another one." Another person said, "It was only a dog." It? It?

On the other hand, many people in trying to make you feel better ask, "So what kind of dog or cat are you going to get now?" They don't realize that for some of us, these dear creatures were gifts from a place where you don't get replacements. It is hard for us to imagine life without them. We still go to feed them or give them a treat or think we should be curling up with them.

I also learned that some people do know what it's like to lose a pet, and they send thoughtful notes of condolence. That surprised me and meant so very much. Some people will ask you to tell your favorite story. And in that moment, your pet comes alive again.

Thank you, Andrea, for giving many of us a chance to remember the beloved creatures we have lost, to honor once again how deeply they let us be human, to appreciate that we can miss them for a lifetime. My thoughts are of you, being there with Leo in his last moments and bringing him to life for us today.

Shortly after this posting, my friend April wrote:

> 🐾 Dear Nance,
>
> Thank you so much for sharing. I just realized why my sister-in-law still has her dog Cindy's ashes in the closet and even brought them with her when she moved to Florida. Cindy was her second dog in thirty years (she has never been blessed with children), and it seemed a bit . . . *odd* is perhaps the only word that comes to mind, that she would not have laid Cindy to rest. I really did not understand her attachment to the ashes, and your sharing has shed much needed light for me, so thank you!

Sometimes we don't understand someone's loss until we hear a friend talk about theirs. No matter how much you care for friends or relatives, it can be hard to comfort them when you may be wondering, and not unkindly, What's the big deal? It may be hard to understand that when we lose a pet, that loss can hurt in ways that are just as deep as losing our best friend.

When You Don't Get the Chance to Say Goodbye
Unfinished feelings

How can you comfort someone who has just lost a loved one without any warning? How do you help people get a sense of closure when they didn't get to say farewell the way they had imagined they would?

Probably one of the nicest things anyone said to us when our mom suddenly died of a heart attack came from my sister Laurie's former camp director (and close family friend), Mrs. Jo. The conversation went something like this:

"I never got to tell her she was going to become a grandma," Laurie cried, regretting that she had planned to tell Mom she was pregnant after she was through her first trimester. She didn't want Mom to worry about her during that often uncertain early pregnancy period. So she had waited to tell her until she got the "all clear" from the doctor. But Mom died before the trimester was up.

"Oh, honey," said Mrs. Jo, looking up into the sky, "She knows. She knows now."

Laurie suddenly got it. Mom probably did know, wherever she was. In that moment, Laurie let go of some of her guilt over not having given Mom the pleasure of anticipating grandmotherhood. "You're right, she knows. I never thought of it that way," she added quietly.

With a few words, from a place of giving grace, Mrs. Jo had acknowledged that Laurie felt sad and even guilty. She offered her a way of holding her grief with a lighter heart of hope. It wasn't preachy. It wasn't "the truth." Instead, Mrs. Jo gave someone she was trying to comfort another way of seeing the situation by listening with her heart.

How else can you comfort people who are feeling the shock of an unexpected loss? They may need to tell you what they wish they had told the person who just died. You might say, "If I were in your shoes right now, I don't know what I would have wished I'd had a chance to tell _____ before she died. If you'd ever like to tell me, I'm willing to listen." Or maybe you could ask whether it would help for them to say or write their unexpressed thoughts to another family member.

After friends have helped you over the initial shock of losing someone without warning, you still want a sense of closure. Friends need to understand that it can take years for you to come to terms with whatever feels unfinished. Ken felt he didn't get to say goodbye to his dad, Charlie, because Ken chose not to speak at his father's funeral. Ten years later, he came to terms with this and wrote a eulogy filled with grit and humor. He shared it with his family and with friends. It was his way of saying, "OK, Dad, now I am ready to honor you and to say goodbye."

Here are some excerpts from Ken's farewell, with some insight he wanted to share about how he was finally able to find a sense of peace with himself.

Who is Charlie Lickel? Charlie is the father to his six children.

He strongly encouraged me to go to college. I was bent on going into the Marines like all my buddies at the time. Dad sat me down one night with a couple of beers, and by daybreak he had me talked into going to college. Looking back, this is the best move I (he) ever made.

He loved people at all levels. I remember him telling me that when you go into a shop, the first person you want to meet is the janitor. When I asked him why, he said that people, no matter what their level, deserve respect. Dad found it hard to express his love. He did it in ways that were not traditional. You could always feel his wanting to express the heart he had. No matter how tough he was, in the end, you always knew he acted in love and appreciation for all.

Especially memorable were his one-liners. My favorite being "Son (to anyone who was young), you've done well for yourself, but you're still a no good piece of s——." And then he would hug you and give you a kiss and say how proud he was of you.

Then Ken explained why he couldn't speak at his father's funeral:

It wasn't for lack of things to say. In fact, I gave the priest a lot to say about my father. I was speaking through him. Why I didn't get up was possibly a fear of not doing it right. Or having someone say I did it wrong. Strange, I knew what to say, but if I knew what I know today about expressing feelings, I would have known that there was no way to do it wrong. No matter what I said or how it came out from me, as long as what I was saying had real feeling associated with it (and it would have), everyone would have felt the love I had for my father, which is all that would have mattered.

If you know people who feel that they didn't get a chance to say farewell—either because of a sudden death or, like Ken, because they didn't know what to say publicly—you can pause to explore what could be holding them back from saying goodbye. When the time is right, they may find a sense of completion by creating a public or private ceremony:

- Releasing long-held thoughts by writing a letter to the person who has died
- Planning a public ceremony to share memories or a celebration supper featuring the person's favorite foods
- Playing a last round of golf on the person's favorite course
- Taking a hike into the mountains where they can have a final "talk"
- Sending out a eulogy as a "years after" testimonial to the spirit of the person they loved

Coming to terms with loss doesn't happen on a schedule. At times, we have to give ourselves—and others—time to let our head catch up with our heart.

It's a Blessing, Really

When death brings relief

DON'T WORRY ABOUT ME; I'LL BE FINE. IT WAS A BLESSING," GRACE SAID, telling her neighbor that her father had finally passed away. "It's better this way," she explained. "He doesn't have to suffer anymore."

What do you say when a friend tells you that the death of a loved one was a blessing? It eliminates the usual response of saying, "I'm so sorry." In this case, the people who've just lost someone they love are feeling more relieved than sorry. They don't have to deal with the midnight calls from the nursing home, the feelings of guilt or inadequacy, the wondering when it will all end.

It's easy to be at a loss for words when a friend tells you that someone's death is a blessing. It helps if you can accept the comment and acknowledge that even so, there are memories to be sifted through, endings to be made, dreams that were realized and ones that will never come true. The survivors are coming to terms with the ending, even if it has been a long time coming.

Maybe the long-expected death feels like an anticlimax. It takes longer for grief to arrive because it has been held in the wings for so long.

You can never assume how someone is feeling in these circumstances. You don't want to be the first to say, "It's a blessing," and you also don't want to be shocked if that's how a family is talking about finally arriving at the end of a difficult journey. On this particular night, Grace doesn't want a hug, and she definitely doesn't want her neighbors to haul up the hill with supper. By listening to the energy behind her words, her friend could tell that she wants to be left alone, to be with her small family, and to organize the flotsam and jetsam of her father's life. Maybe they will tell stories and remember old times with a smile and an ache. Mostly they will come to terms with a hole in the fabric of their lives that also reminds them of the loss, years earlier, of their mother. It is a completion when both parents are gone. It is an odd moment to realize, for the first time, that you are no longer anyone's child.

It may be hard to ever see someone's death as a blessing. It may be contrary to the way we were raised or to the way we see life. However, if we want to comfort someone who feels relieved that the end has finally come, it helps if we can accept that view and give it grace, even if we don't think we could ever feel that way. We might say, "It seems that his death has ended a difficult time for all of you. I imagine that it will take time to adjust to its finally being over."

How *do* you give grace to others' feeling that death could be a blessing? By accepting their experience as valid and by not judging that they should feel any other way than the way they do.

Take a Friend to Lunch
Writing the obituary

S HE WASN'T EVEN SICK. WHY WAS SHE ASKING ME TO WRITE HER OBITUARY? This was just too strange. Don't you know, though, it was a good thing she had asked me to do it, because a few months later, without warning, she was gone.

Mom lived alone on top of a mountain in North Carolina. One night, she phoned and we chatted for a while about this and that. I can't remember the bits and pieces of the conversation. Then she got to the point of her call. "Nance," she said, "I want you to do something for me. It's pretty simple, but important, and because you are the writer in the family, I'd like you to write it."

"OK, Mom. What's up?" I asked.

"I've thought about this and I don't want you to argue with me," she said. "I'd like you to write my obituary while I'm alive so I can make sure it says what I want it to say."

Well, as you can imagine, this wasn't your usual Sunday night "Mom call." I guess there aren't many nights when you are prepared to say, "Sure, fine,

Mom, I'll write your obit." They don't give you this assignment in tenth-grade English class, though maybe it would be a good assignment for us to undertake as adults. I'll bet that not many of us have taken a crack at doing this while our folks were around and still healthy.

My assignment was to convey how important friends were to Mom. Since they lived nearby, and none of us kids did, we knew that they meant a lot to her. Her friends could be right there to help her with the things in life that can overwhelm you when you're living alone—you don't feel well, your house burns down, you have an operation, you wreck your car on the ice—the kinds of things after which it's hard to go home alone at night to an empty house. This is how she wanted to be remembered:*

❧ Take a Friend to Lunch

Eileen Guilmartin has asked friends and family to honor her memory in a special way. Although she loved flowers and dogs and cats and community causes, today she'd like you to take time out for someone else who is special to you. Don't wait until it's too late. Don't let yourself run up any more excuses. Call up a friend and go to lunch. Do it now. You don't want to wish that you'd done something so simple as to spend an hour with someone you care about. One day it may be too late. So why wait? Honoring friendship: it's how you can leave a little legacy for you and for me.

The most important lesson wasn't about having the obituary written ahead of time, although it did save us one more thing to deal with during the

---

*Newspapers may edit submissions, as ours did when we submitted what we'd written. This is the version my mother approved.

initial shock of our mother's death. The most important thing was that Mom and I got to talk about what she valued in life and how she wanted to be remembered.

Conversations about death can open new doors to people you love while they are alive. Sharing stories can help you get started when you are at a loss for words. When two sisters heard the story about me writing my mother's obituary, the younger one told me that even though she was perfectly healthy, for years she had been wanting to talk about her eventual death to her sister. "It's a conversation I've wanted to have but haven't known how to start," she explained. "Your story has given us a chance to talk. My next step will be to share my obituary with my children. To let them know that it's written and to talk about the service I'd like. I feel so relieved to have had a chance to get this out in the open. It's so simple once you get started."

Your conversation could start out sounding something like this: "I haven't known how to bring this up before, but there's something I'd like to talk about. I hate the thought of my family having to write my obituary in the hours after I've died. I thought it would be great to have it done now while I'm alive. It would be taken care of, and everyone would know this ahead of time. Would you consider writing my obituary for me? If you want help getting started, I could ask you to remind people that one thing that was important to me was . . . If you want to write something up, we can go over it together. Feel free to talk to _____ for ideas."

Friends and families are learning that sometimes, when you don't think you'll know what to say about people you love, you can say exactly the right things. Creating this very special message while they are alive can be a way to bring friends and families closer together before they are gathered around a casket or an urn.

Oh, Damn! Did Anybody Bring a Knife?

🖎 *Scattering ashes*

WHAT DO YOU SAY TO YOUR BROTHERS AND SISTERS WHEN IT'S TIME TO scatter the ashes of your parents? That's the situation our family faced. When the time came, we realized not only did we not know what to say to each other, but we didn't quite know how to handle something that had seemed pretty simple—it's just scattering ashes, right?

There we were, at the edge of the ocean, absolutely certain that we could handle the situation. After all, we'd made it through the most uncomfortable parts of the event—strangers coming up to us before the funeral service. Listening to the minister we barely knew talking about our dad as a man who cared about justice. Well, yes, he did. Yet for all his years of standing up for important causes, he died in a simple way—eating coffee ice cream for breakfast. Heart just stopped beating. Died alone. No fuss. No last-minute attempts to save him. Probably a gasp and then he was gone.

The strange thing is that he died about two weeks before three of his four kids were going to see him in a rare reunion. We'd planned to fly in to Miami to be together. Too late. And now all four of us were together at the edge of the ocean. Waiting for the moment when one of us would have the nerve to open the box that held his ashes. To scatter them into the sea. You know, like you read about in books or hear friends say they've done? Scatter the ashes.*

Sounds comforting, doesn't it? As if for a moment you can hold the person you loved once again. Then, in the next moment, you are letting him go toward God or spirits or whatever lies beyond.

There we were. Ready to scatter the ashes. Feeling the heebie-jeebies and wondering, "Is this OK with God and the spirits or what?" No rule book. No instructions on how to do this. Just guessing that you open the cardboard box of ashes and, with great dignity, send the remains into space. We unseal the box to discover a thick plastic bag. No problem, we think, just tear it open.

If you haven't ever scattered ashes, here's a vital fact most people don't know: there's a law that requires that the bag with the ashes in it be hermetically sealed so that it does not open unexpectedly while in transit—like through the mail.

We couldn't get the bag open.

This isn't something anyone had warned us about. Someone had given us the good advice that you don't need to buy a $200 urn if you are going to scatter the ashes, which is why we didn't have an urn and never bothered to open the box. But no one had advised us to bring a pocket knife to the ceremony!

---

*Most states have regulations about scattering ashes. You may want to consult your local funeral home for guidance.

In the end, we sawed open the bag with a sharp rock we found on the ground.

Once we got the bag open, however, we made a new discovery: the ashes of the person you love don't exactly scatter; they pour, like the finest pumice sand you've ever seen, and there may be bone fragments, too. The ashes do not float in the wind like you've seen in the movies or in your imagination.

Four years later, we were out on a borrowed boat on the lake where we'd grown up as kids. It was February. In North Carolina. It was cold. My sister, three months pregnant, was shivering as we reached the middle of the lake we all loved, a good place to pour Mom's ashes. We had learned from our experience with Dad that we didn't need an urn and that the ashes wouldn't scatter; they'd pour. We knew what to expect, or so we thought. We still weren't sure whether we were allowed to be doing this in a public place. But there we were.

When we went to open the box with the bag of ashes in it, we had a moment of much needed though unexpected laughter when my brother said, "Hey, Mom, you sure are heavier than Dad." We couldn't help but laugh, and the laughter helped us relax a bit and not feel so weird about what we were doing. We felt closer to Mom by not pretending that she wasn't who she was.

We got the box open. Then one of us said, "Oh, damn! Did anyone bring a knife this time?" We laughed again, remembering what we'd gone through with Dad.

"Hey, you don't think I was going to go through that again, do you?" my brother said. To our relief, he snapped out his little pocket knife and neatly slit open the bag and we each poured a little of Mom into the lake where she had spent so many happy times.

When you are going to scatter the ashes of someone you love, you don't want surprises. You don't want someone to suddenly ask, "Did anybody bring a knife?" You don't want to resort to finding a sharp rock and sawing open the heat-sealed plastic bag. However, if you find yourself in the midst of the unexpected, as we did, somehow you will manage and you'll realize that no one is ever really completely prepared to cope with all of the ceremonies involved in letting go of someone you love.

No matter what happens, you will find your own way to release the spirit of the one you love into the earth or the sea or, as one of my friends did, out on the golf course at her father's favorite hole. Perhaps you will sense that the person you love is probably smiling at you in this moment even as you feel weird, even as you wonder if he can hear you or see you. For in that moment, your relationship is transformed because you really, really get it—your loved one isn't in his body anymore, isn't resting neatly in a coffin somewhere, but is literally pouring through your hands into some other part of the earth where the ashes and the dust can mingle and become something new.

Coming to terms with death also taught me another lesson: I wish I'd known not to rush. Nothing can prepare you for that call from the mortuary when you are asked to give permission for someone you love to be cremated. When Mom died and the mortuary called to get her body released, the thought of her lying bare and cold on a slab somewhere was too much for me to handle. Without thinking, I said, "Sure, go ahead."

Imagine my horror when three days later, my sister flew into town and said, "Where's Mom?"

"What do you mean?" I asked. "She's at the mortuary; they have her ashes."

"Oh, no," Laurie cried. "I wanted to say goodbye." It hadn't even crossed my mind that she might want to see Mom's body or that it would be of comfort to her. These are the kinds of mistakes one can make when handling grief and the ceremonies of death—responding to relatives, friends, and strangers who, while offering to help you, may actually need to be comforted as well.

There is no dress rehearsal for these ceremonies, which often get made up as you go along. However embarrassing it is to relate this misstep on my part, I wanted to share it with you because I would not want any other family member to go through what my sister felt when she realized she could not say good-bye the way she would have wished. I am blessed that even though she was disappointed, she graciously understood that I wasn't perfect. Just her sister.

Best-Laid Plans

🐚 *When last wishes clash with the needs of the living*

I F THERE'S ONE THING THAT DEALING WITH DEATH TEACHES YOU, IT IS THE art of compromise. Even the best-laid plans don't always turn out the way you intended. Claire shared a story that might help families avoid the predicament she found herself in after her mother passed away.*

> 🐚 Mother had died, leaving instructions for her ashes to be scattered by me, my sister, and my dad at a special place she loved by the sea. Trouble was, upon hearing the news of her death, relatives and friends wanted to attend the ceremony. They planned to fly in from several states to be part of saying goodbye to Mother. The problem for us was that she had left clear instructions that she wanted no

*Sarah York's book *Remembering Well: Rituals for Celebrating Life and Mourning Death* is an extraordinary resource to help families and friends create healing ceremonies for many kinds of loss.

public fuss made about her; she wanted a simple ceremony with the three of us scattering her ashes and saying our private goodbyes.

What were we to do? Relatives assumed that they could take part in the farewells and were making plans. How could we hurt their feelings by telling them about Mother's wishes? Should we ignore her wishes and keep everyone happy, or should we tell them her wishes and upset them?

You might like to know what we decided.

A week before the announced ceremony date, on one of those soft, misty evenings so familiar to anyone who has experienced Cape Cod, we placed Mother's ashes into three white satin bags reverently created for the purpose, and we drove toward the sea. Because the four of us were taking our last trip together, we paused occasionally at some of her most cherished places and reminisced. Surprisingly, we were comforted by sights and sounds that had been integral parts of our lives.

Upon reaching our destination, we found the shore deserted, and the only sounds were those of small waves lapping against the sand. But there was something else—the distinctive sound of a halyard gently rapping against a mast. But this could not be . . . no boats were permitted in this area . . . yet there she was, a white sailboat, sails furled, not moored but not moving, showing no lights and emitting no sound other than an intermittent almost musical tapping. And so we set Mother's earthly remains free in the way that she had wished us to do, witnessed only by us three and the misty boat playing sea music.

To enable the other relatives to say goodbye, we perpetrated a fraud. You see, I figured we could gather some ashes from the fireplace, the woodstove, the grille, throw in some phosphate granules and other substances to create an acceptable substitute for the real thing, and hope for the best. We would not have hurt our relatives' feelings by excluding them from the "ceremony." For all intents and purposes, it would proceed as planned, and no one would know the difference.

We thought that we had it all handled. The relatives arrived. We piled into cars and went back out to the ocean. The three of us took our new bags of ashes, left the group, waded into the water, and began to pour the ashes into the sea. We felt foolish but also felt that we'd done the right thing for all concerned. Even Dad, not the most expressive of humans, said under his breath to Mother, "Well, my dear, better twice than not at all." And then we looked down in the water where we were pouring the ashes, and it had started to bubble and froth. Not just a little, but in an ever-widening circle, as if something were rising up from under the sea.

We couldn't figure out at first what was happening. Maybe there was something in the water or wave action. We didn't know. So we frantically started to try to smooth out the bubbles. As what had happened began to dawn on us, we started to laugh. We knew that Mother's laughter was heartiest of all. Obviously, something that we'd incorporated into our mixture was making the water froth and bubble. We were relieved that our relatives back on land couldn't tell exactly what was happening, and when we returned, they mistook our tears of laughter for tears of sadness. In the end, we knew that Mother (and God) had definitely had the last word on our activities. She had approved, and no one was the wiser.

I'm telling you this story because I want people to see what ridiculous lengths families sometimes have to go to when loved ones pass away without informing others about how they wish to have their passing honored. Fortunately, Mother made her wishes clear to us, but we were totally unprepared for the unexpected response to her death from others. Having to choose between honoring the requests of the person who has died and helping those who are still living come to terms with the loss only adds to the already overwhelming grief.

Please talk to your family and friends now. Don't leave it to them to try to figure out what they should do when you are no longer there to help them decide. If you feel that you cannot talk about it, leave written instructions for them to follow. You cannot leave a more thoughtful gift to those who are left behind.

If you do make your wishes known to friends and family, give them the benefit of the doubt. They might find themselves in a situation, as Claire's story revealed, of not quite being able to follow your instructions to the letter. And if you are the ones finding yourselves having to compromise, it helps if you can give yourself a break and leave a little room for the unexpected. It's the way life works, just to remind us that we are not always in control of how it begins or how it ends.

When Mom Leaves

A gift of poetry

SOMETIMES THE WORDS OF COMFORT WE OFFER CAN BE OUR OWN. SOME-times they can be written by others. When a friend's mother died of a heart attack, there was no way I could reach her. I wrote this poem for her to have as something to turn to after she got back home. To my surprise, many families have read the poem at graveside ceremonies, memorials, and farewell services. I've included it here for anyone to use or perhaps to inspire you to write your own verse. I don't consider myself a poet. Yet maybe at certain times it's the sen-timent that counts, and that's what brings comfort to another who is grieving.

WHEN MOM LEAVES

When she is gone
in a flash,
unbidden,
there is a loss

like no other.
You see
when Mom leaves
there is a center missing
as if the universe
has lost its gravity.

Everything,
everything falls apart
for a while
until the universe
of our lives
finds a way
back to center.
And somehow
while there is no force
holding it together
the way it was—
somehow
we are
whole again
in
the
middle
of
it
all.

After the Funeral

Appreciating behind-the-scenes responsibilities

A FTER THE CASSEROLE DISHES HAVE BEEN RETURNED, THE FLOWERS HAVE been planted at the grave, the condolence notes have been read, what can you do to provide support in the many tasks that lie ahead? One way to show you care is to appreciate what the mourners are going through as they make decisions no one ever taught them how to make. This is where having compassion can make a difference and where you can also help by understanding that they may or may not want company as they sift through an avalanche of memories and to-do lists.

What kinds of decisions are they facing? First of all, most of us aren't prepared to go through other people's closets, medicine cabinets, or desks—and what do you do with the laundry? The food in the cabinets? The gifts that had been bought but not yet given? The mementos that had meaning known only to them? What do you do when you come across old photos of people you don't know? Are they people you should have known? Do they hold keys to better understanding the person who just died? Does reading this list overwhelm you? Well, that's how it can feel when you are managing the aftermath of a death: overwhelming.

Then there is even more to do. Do we call the people listed in his address book to tell them that he has passed away? What do we say when the person on the other end of the line, upon hearing this news, exclaims, "Oh, no, he *can't* be dead."

What do we save as a keepsake of the one who is gone? What goes to friends and family? What goes to charity, what goes to the dump, and what gets sold? And what about all the legal requirements of forms, taxes to deal with, death certificates, bills to be settled? Few people realize how much time it takes to deal with the business of a person's death, even when there is no quarrel about a will or about the distribution of possessions.

Then there are all the decisions you have to make about what to do about someone's pets, dealing with unanswered correspondence, sending back things ordered by mail. You are picking up the many loose threads of a person's private life. You spend days feeling like a voyeur, trespassing in a place where you don't belong, and yet it is a time when trespassing is the only way you can put the person's life and death in order.

When our mom died, people gave us practical advice. Someone suggested that when it came to dividing up possessions, we make a list of our top picks. If two of us wanted the same thing, we'd work it out. They told us that in the end, our relationships as siblings had to outlast the objects. Things, they said, could always be broken or stolen or lost, while what remained of our family had to live on. We hit a few rough spots, but we made it just fine. We appreciated the advice.

Someone else suggested that you could sell used clothes at the secondhand clothing shop and donate the proceeds to a local shelter or charity. Another person helped organize a garage sale so that we would not have to watch as Mom's things were removed from the house. Several people volunteered to take her pets because we weren't in a position to do that—we were so grateful.

One lesson we learned the hard way, and we wished we'd known it then: you will come across mementos that you aren't sure whether or not you should keep. Things like boxes of letters to your mom from a grandparent, scrapbooks from before you were born, pictures from trips taken without you. To our regret, we tossed a lot of these things. Why didn't we save them? Lots of reasons. We didn't have a place to store them. They conflicted with our memories. We felt that these private scraps weren't for our eyes. We were on overload and couldn't even begin to consider how valuable they would be to our children, or to us, years later. What you can suggest to others facing this kind of "overwhelm" is to keep a few boxes marked "Sort later." And then do it—years later.

Here are some responses to questions raised in this story:

- *What do you give away?* Objects that had special meaning can bring comfort to close friends, many of whom would never ask you to give them something but who will be touched if you do (a book, a piece of jewelry, a memento, tools, a photograph, a plant).

- *How do you call all the people in the address book?* Take your time, ask a friend or relative to help you do this, send notes, and don't try to do it all yourself.

- *What about bills, legal estate forms, taxes, and such?* Get advice from more than one source you trust. Take your time, and keep family members informed if you are the executor of the estate. Don't expect that you will do everything right—few of us have any training in how to make these kinds of decisions.

- *What about old photos in which you don't recognize the people?* Save them—someday you may have a chance to identify the people or learn more about the history of that time by researching the photograph.

After the funeral, after the ashes have been scattered, the songs have been sung, the condolence notes have been stashed away, and the will has been read, that's when the real digging up and burial begins. It can take weeks, months, even years before the dust settles. There may be practical things you can do to help some relatives clear out their memories. Others may need time to do it on their own but will appreciate that you understand all the difficult decisions they are making. Knowing that you know this will give them comfort.

When a Young Child Dies

A parent's bewilderment lingers

PARENTS NEVER EXPECT TO OUTLIVE THEIR CHILDREN. WHEN THEY DO, MANY ask, "Why? Was I a bad parent? Did I do something wrong? Why wasn't it me who died instead of my child?"

Sometimes the siblings who survive ask similar questions.

Lynn's brother had died decades ago. During all of those years, her mother hadn't talked much about his death to friends or family. One day, Lynn asked her mother if she would be willing to talk to me because I wanted to include a story in this book about how to comfort families coping with the death of a child.

Her mother began by explaining that her son was the youngest of the family. He was fourteen years old. The day he died, he was playing with ropes in a tree. It had been raining. Something went wrong with the knots. He died of a broken neck. The doctor said it was an accident. At the moment this happened, his mom, who had four other children, was visiting shut-ins at a nearby nursing home. She still remembers what one of the eighty-year-old residents told her that day, not knowing, of course, that it would be the last day of life for a young child.

"The woman I was visiting said, 'You know, I'd like to die today. I'm ready to die. I don't know why I'm still alive.' To this day, I think about the irony of that moment. Here was someone who was ready to be released, and instead, my son was taken."

At first, I thought she was expressing regret for not having been home when her son was playing. But then I paused and realized that she was saying that it was ironic, perhaps unfair, that the one who died that day was someone who she thought couldn't possibly have been ready to die. Not that day. Not that young. Not that way.

Tuning in to the bewilderment she seemed to be expressing, I wondered what anyone could possibly have done to comfort her. That's why I asked, "What did people do or say that helped you through those difficult times?"

"Oh, I don't know," she said quite honestly. "I was so numb for so long, I'm not sure I noticed. I don't hold anything against anybody. How can you know what to do or say when someone's child is taken so suddenly? One thing I would tell people is to please not say that you know how someone feels. How can you possibly know how I feel when I'm so numb that even I don't know how I feel?"

Lynn's mom continued, "I would also like people to know that somehow we do get through these things. Day to day, hour to hour, there are plenty of times when you think you won't get through and don't want to go on. Then the memories come back about the delight you felt in your child. It is hard for a while to have hopes and dreams again."

Earlier she had mentioned that she had four other children. It seemed important to acknowledge that while she was grieving the loss of one child, she had to continue being a parent to four children. Maybe there was something she wanted to communicate to other grieving parents. "Somehow you managed to raise your other four children," I commented. "What helped you do that?"

"Well," she remembered, "we made sure to spend extra time with each child before he or she went off to college. We wanted to make sure each one felt special. The Friday night before my son died, he was marching in the band. There was a moment I just looked at him and had strong feelings of closeness. I meant to tell him this, but I guess I never did. We don't communicate that well as a family sometimes, but after he died, it became even more important for me to let the children know how much I love them."

"Does it help to have any of his old friends stop by?" I asked, wondering what had been of comfort to her as the years passed.

"Oh, yes, yes, it's wonderful when they do," she said, and I could almost feel the smile on her face when she told me this. "One of his friends, Mike, brings me homemade guava jelly each year. Mike comes and we talk. It helps to have someone who really knew him. We can share memories. It keeps his spirit alive. I don't know how other people would feel about being visited by their lost child's friends, but for me, it is very helpful.

"I'm not sure what lessons I've learned from this that I can pass on to others," she murmured. "Sometimes I wonder if I was a good mother," she said, as she talked about what it was like to have raised four children while also keeping her husband company in their grief. "I'm determined, though," she said, "to keep trying to get my kids to talk about my son's death even though they don't want to after all these years. We have to learn to communicate someday." She also talked about a lot of seemingly unrelated things, including that her son's death hadn't stopped her from continuing to visit the elders in the nursing home and that her dad had been a doctor.

Listening quietly as she wandered from one topic to another, it seemed to me that she was trying to make sense of what had happened. I sensed that there was more to the story because she was hesitant to draw any conclusions. She didn't blame herself, her son, God, or the weather, but something didn't seem quite right to her, and I felt that she needed time to speak the pieces of the puzzle out loud without being told how they all fit together.

As I've said many times in this book, healing conversations are very much about being with others with the right amount of energy at the right time for them. You don't have to tie up all the loose ends in one conversation. Sometimes your role is to open a door to more conversation either later with you or perhaps with others. Having spoken so much after a long silence, it was a time for Lynn's mother to hear her own thoughts out loud and then let her feelings settle. It wasn't necessary for me to ask more questions, even though there were more to ask.

Just talking out loud, without feeling that she had to have everything all figured out, was the first step toward the healing her daughter had hoped for. But there was another step that helped shake loose some of what had remained unspoken. It happened when she read a written version of what she had told me that day. Lynn said that when her mother had a chance to quietly read the story, it gave her a chance to realize that she was now ready to share something she'd never told anyone.

After reading the words she had spoken about her son's death, Lynn's mother was able to tell her daughter that she didn't see how her son's death could have been an accident. Even though the doctor determined that the boy had slipped while playing with the ropes, she had wondered then, and still does today, whether or not that was really what happened. "Perhaps he was unhappy," she thought. "Perhaps he was afraid of letting his parents down—he'd been kicked off the football team a few days before. He was fourteen—an emotionally challenging time," she said softly.

This is an example of how powerful the practice of rephrasing can be—in this case, the words were rephrased to the person in writing because that gave her time to reflect. You can give the gift of rephrasing (during the conversation) by telling others, in your own words, what you think you heard them say about their difficult circumstances. Or you can do it in writing. Letting people hear or see what you think you heard them say gives them a chance to realize what they may have left unspoken.

I chose to rephrase her words in writing, rather than during our phone call, because it seemed that she needed time to come to terms with the doubts she had about how her son died. How did I know this? Because she wasn't quite ready to speak her fear out loud—the fear that her son had taken his own life. She needed time to find the words. And most likely I shouldn't be the one she should tell, even though I sensed it was what she most needed to say. It wasn't time yet. Her first step was to talk to someone who she felt wouldn't have any reason to judge her or wouldn't try to tell her that her fears were foolish or unfounded.

A few days later, Lynn called to share what had happened after her Mom had had time to think about what she was now ready to tell her family. "I let Mom talk and talk. I didn't interrupt her. I learned that Mom's inability to heal was connected with her not voicing a deeply held fear that perhaps my brother had committed suicide. I never knew she had these thoughts. I'm sure each of us in the family has wondered about it, but we never discussed it openly. Maybe now all of us can."

Parents who have lost a child may need to talk to someone who won't judge them, who won't try to talk them out of how they are feeling. Who will, for a while, let them wonder if the child's death was in any way their fault, even if it wasn't. They need to be able to express their feelings and not be rushed into feeling something else, even if that would make everyone else feel better. Some parents who have experienced the death of a young child say that it is hard to stop blaming themselves. It's not a feeling that is easy to get over, even if the evidence surrounding the child's death doesn't point to them. As Lynn explained, "We'll never know what happened the day my brother died. But we've learned that if we don't talk, we can become distant."

Lynn didn't try to talk her mother out of her fears. She allowed her mom to finally express what had stayed hidden for many years—a secret of sorts that had kept the family from doing the one thing her mom vowed they would now learn how to do: communicate.

Frail Submarines

🐚 *When someone chooses suicide*

VAIL WAS TRYING TO COME TO TERMS WITH WHY HER COUSIN AND A FRIEND had ended their lives. Her father had died several months earlier, after fighting a long battle to stay alive. After watching him fight to live, it was hard for her to understand why these two other people she loved hadn't asked for help. She also wondered why no one had been able to see they were so troubled. She wrote an e-mail about being overwhelmed:

> 🐚 I'm feeling frail, very weak—like the wind has been completely knocked out of me. I can feel it in my body. I'm hunched inward, shoulders forward—protecting my heart. My breathing is shallow. I'm tired. Very tired. And I'm giving room to myself to just be—tub baths, phone calls, visitors, or silence, whatever I need.

I wondered whether I should call or write. What is she able to hear right now, especially since she is telling me she feels so fragile? Sometimes we may want to call friends to learn a little more about what they are most troubled by—perhaps it's not what they've said first; it may be what they haven't expressed. After calling her, I wrote this note:

Dear Vail,

You wrote about your cousin Brenda and your friend Harry ending their lives and about the frail sadness that you are letting yourself feel over their deaths. You say that it seemed before she took her life, Brenda was OK—happy. You wrote, "We don't know what lies hidden in people." An hour ago I called you because I didn't want to simply write you a letter—I wanted to listen to you first.

One thing we didn't talk about tonight was how easy it is for people to miss the signs that someone is thinking of taking his or her life. When I was in that place, no one—not friends, family, or spouse—had a clue about how deep my emotional submarine had gone diving. Some of us are able to be one person on the outside and a different person buried alive on the inside, unable to find a way out. This is how we feel: no way out. We can feel this way even when to you our life may appear to be going along just fine. Unfortunately some people will choose to dive into inner space where they can disappear, and no one can find them there, unless they want to accept your help to reach the surface again.

To me, part of being human is to choose life, not be resigned to it, obligated to it, or "shoulded" into it. Choosing life is a way for us to reaffirm that we are living a life worthy of who we were born to be. This is why, every once in a while, I find it is a good experience for me to stop and think about how I am spending—investing, actually—my life's time.

I am so sorry that your cousin and friend are not here to grace your life, or ours, with their physical presence. You said it is hard for you to understand why they could not see past the pain of their current circumstances. Sometimes it is in someone's leaving us that we wake up and are forced to live life more consciously, with more questions, more appreciation, more commitment.

When someone you know makes the decision to take her or his own life, you can feel sad, bewildered, guilty, and even angry that the person did not ask for your help. People's view of suicide can be shaped by their life's experiences—just as Vail's inability to comprehend why her friends ended their lives was affected by having seen her dad fight to stay alive, right until the final day of his life.

It's not always easy to know what to say to friends who have lost someone to suicide. It's a good time to listen first, either for their questions or for what they need to say. When someone tells you a loved one has committed suicide, first pause to breathe and feel your own feelings. Give yourself a moment to connect with your own sense of loss or anger before trying to say anything. It's a good time to acknowledge that perhaps you are at a loss for words but that you care for your friend. You might gently ask what your friend would like you to know about how he is coming to terms with what happened. You aren't after the gory details of how the person died. You are trying to let him know that you are prepared to listen to whatever he needs to express.

Here's an example of what happened one day when my friend Bill told me that his son had recently taken his own life. "What would you like me to know about your son?" I asked. Bill talked about how he wanted friends and family to honor his son's choice. "If I feel his death is in vain, then so was his life," Bill explained. "I miss my son. I wish he was still alive, but I am choosing to honor his memory by honoring the choice he made. His spirit is free—it is our pain and our perceptions of his death that are so difficult."

What if your mind starts reacting to what your friend is asking of you? You could think to yourself, How on earth could a father say such a thing—honor his child's choice to die? That's against my religion, my beliefs, my whole sense of responsibility as a parent. Where is his outrage? His guilt? How could he say such a thing? It's very human to have this kind of reaction when someone says something you aren't prepared to hear. What can you do if your inner judge starts driving you down this road? Pause; take a few slow breaths. Remember your commitment: to be there for your friend. Remember, this isn't about you right now. As hard as it may be, try to remember that you are there to have a healing conversation, not to advance your point of view or to challenge anyone else's.

Had I rushed to comfort Bill out of my own discomfort, I would have missed hearing how he was coming to terms with his grief. Often people will let you know what they need by giving you signals that all they want is for you to listen—they don't want you to resolve anything. This is where it takes a little courage to be with people in their loss. You have to be willing to let them take you where they are feeling, even if you don't think that's how you would feel if this happened to you.

One way to help yourself be a nonjudgmental listener could be to prepare yourself before you write, call, or visit your friend. First, you could talk to a friend, a spiritual counselor, or a family member to help you get perspective. Or you could privately write down some of your thoughts and feelings just to get them out of your system.

When trying to support someone who is experiencing a sudden or tragic death, it also helps if we can accept one important thing: it's not up to us to make sense of it. As Bill requested of his friends, it would not comfort him if they tried to make what seems wrong, wrong. Asking us to honor the choice to end one's life may be asking a lot. It reminds us that giving the gift of supporting someone in pain may take us to places where later on, when we're alone, we'll ask ourselves a lot of questions about our own beliefs. But when we are trying to comfort people, it is a time for us to support them in their beliefs. Sometimes the best we can do is ask if it would be OK to give them a hug.

When Tragedy Inspires Action

Responding to a sudden death

HOW DO YOU TRANSFORM TRAGEDY INTO POSITIVE ACTION?

Dennis Kauff was a television reporter. He was thirty-one years old when he died, after being slammed into at an intersection by a drunk driver. An adult had bought beer for two underage boys. They were driving over eighty miles per hour when they ran the red light, hitting Dennis's car. It was November 1985.

Within hours, I was called to WBZ-TV in Boston, the television station where I worked as the director of communications and editorials. Dennis was one of our best reporters—he always found a way to put a little bit of heart into his news stories. I was asked to help our staff deal with the shock, the grief, and—ironically—the media.

We were angry and hurt. We vowed that Dennis's death would not be in vain.

271

We knew we had to do more than broadcast traditional public service announcements saying, "Don't drink and drive." We asked ourselves, "What could we do that would ensure that Dennis's death would inspire a legacy to keep others from dying at the hands of a drunk driver?"

Fortunately for us, the Harvard School of Public Health saw an opportunity. With Dennis's death, the school felt that the time was right to approach us to discuss new ways to prevent drunk driving deaths. Jay Winsten, one of the deans at the school, told us that the media and the public didn't seem to understand that campaigning for tougher drunk driving penalties wasn't keeping drunk drivers from killing people. At that time, most jurors didn't want to impose stiff penalties because they would think, There but for the grace of God go I. Apparently, jurors also didn't think that drinking and driving should be punishable by jail time.

We had to stop to think about what the real problem was. Until that moment, all of us—the public, the media, and the legislature—had thought that the way to stop people from drinking and driving was to admonish them not to do it. Research showed that many drunk drivers who were arrested were alcoholics. Trying to convince them not to drink and drive was almost futile. We had to try another route. We focused instead on the social drinker. We realized that we needed to shift the culture so that there was a social stigma attached to drinking and driving. There also had to be a new norm that defined a socially acceptable role for the abstainer. In addition, addressing the message "Who's driving tonight?" to a group of two or more people meant we'd put it on their interpersonal, social agenda.

We researched the drunk driving laws in our state, the country, and the world. We knew that since the 1930s, Scandinavians believed it was totally unacceptable to ever drink and drive. They had tough laws, but it seemed that friends and family played an even more powerful role in making it unacceptable to even think of drinking and driving. Closer to home, we discovered that the Washington, D.C., Regional Alcohol Program had done a three-month campaign in which it partnered with a few restaurants to offer free nonalcoholic drinks to the person in a party who would promise to drive everyone home and not to drink. They called it the designated driver program. We decided to take this idea one step further and create the first statewide campaign with our state's restaurant association, because it was the bars and restaurants that were liable if they served too much alcohol to a patron. We broadcast TV and radio messages to explain the designated driver concept to viewers, and waiters and waitresses were carefully trained to ask groups of people, "Who's the designated driver tonight?"

When we first began this program, it was a pilot project launched only in Massachusetts with the help of the Harvard School of Public Health and the Massachusetts Restaurant Association. All of us were taking a risk, including Westinghouse Broadcasting, which owned our television station. We wondered whether it would work and whether people who were not driving would start drinking too much, causing a whole new problem. But after sticking with it for a year, the program was a success. It spread nationwide after Jay began to take the message to Hollywood. He convinced television writers and producers to start including the designated driver concept in their scripts. We'll never forget the night when Sam, the bartender on the popular television program "Cheers," asked a group of customers, "Who's the designated driver here?"

Many ordinary people have undertaken extraordinary efforts to make a difference after something in their lives went terribly wrong. Judy Shepard is dedicating her life to educating people about the high cost of hate. Her son,

Matthew, was beaten to death for being gay. When Nancy Bostley died of cancer, her family collaborated with their YMCA to start Nancamp, a local, subsidized outreach program for children and families affected by cancer. The Forget-Me-Not Foundation was created to help families of brain-injured patients. It was founded after the family of Nan Zobel couldn't get the help they needed to cope with the aftereffects of a serious brain injury.

When friends and families set out to create a living legacy in the wake of a tragedy, few of us know how much work it will take. Our success is made possible because families, officials, banks, lawmakers, the media, and strangers pitch in to help. We take risks. We learn how to communicate new and sometimes unpopular messages to the public. We hang in there for the long haul. We take comfort in doing something. We learn that we never know what we are capable of doing until something very painful touches the core of our being—inspiring us to action.

Grief Unburied

Sorrow returns in waves

G RIEF IS LIKE A WAVE," THE COUNSELOR SAID TO THE TELEVISION AUDI-
ence. "It comes and goes in its own time."

His words hit me in a way I hadn't expected as the televised memorial service began for the six Massachusetts' firefighters killed while trying to save the
lives of people they thought were in an abandoned warehouse.

For days, the news media had told the story: Cold storage warehouse.
Abandoned. Except word came the night of the fire that two people, two
homeless people, might be living there somewhere in the cold of winter. More
than two dozen firefighters rushed into the building that night in an effort to
rescue two people who might or might not be there. It didn't matter to the
firefighters whether the people they were searching for were rich or poor,
homeless or not. Their job was to save lives—any lives. But the fire got out of
control. There were few windows to break to vent the thick smoke. The cap-
tain decided to call all the men out of the building because the fire had become

too dangerous. But after evacuating the flaming building, two men did not answer at roll call. Word came that they were running out of oxygen, they were trapped somewhere.

The firefighters' code says to rescue your own. Two by two, they rushed in to save their buddies who were lost in the smoke, their air supply running out. Hours later came the news that six men had died. Six partners in a brotherhood where, as one fireman said, "One doesn't fail. Two fail. Because you always go in with your buddy."

Like many others, I tuned in to the televised memorial service. I was curious to learn what compelled tens of thousands to make their way to Worcester, Massachusetts, a medium-sized city of old mills and traditional values struggling to turn the corner into the twenty-first century. It turns out that nearly thirty thousand firefighters from around the world traveled there, at their own expense, to stand silent vigil in memory of six fallen heroes. Not three hundred, not three thousand, but thirty thousand firefighters from as far away as California, Hawaii, Australia, and Ireland. Two-hundred and fifty would come from Vermont alone. The president and vice president were coming. All to honor heroes in a profession many of us perhaps take for granted as they quietly go about responding to false alarms and towering infernos.

The memorial service made one thing very clear: *grief is timeless.* That's the phrase one of the commentators offered to the at-home audience. I knew this, intellectually, but it had never hit me quite so hard as when, tuning in to watch an event about other people's grief, it unexpectedly unlocked my own. Triggered by the stories of life cut short, of seventeen children who would now be growing up without fathers, the stories hit home about my own life and the lives of those I'd lost. How many others out there watching this mournful procession were also feeling old losses anew? Perhaps this has happened for you when you read or see the story of someone else's death—whether someone famous, such as Princess Diana, or an unknown child of war. You may be reminded of your own unexpected loss.

No, my father wasn't a firefighter, he was just my dad, but he died before we were ready to let him go. Same with my mom. Same with my friend Dennis. All gone many years ago. When some incident reminds us of our loss, we say to ourselves, You'd think the grief would be over by now. The memorial service was one more reminder that grief isn't something you bury like a casket or something you scatter like ashes. It is, just like the television commentator described, something that comes in waves. Sometimes those waves tumble you about, leaving you disoriented. Sometimes those waves of grief pull you down like a surging undertow when you least expect it. Sometimes they throw you up on shore exhausted. And sometimes they hold you in the cradle of their force, gently carrying you toward the sand.

In his remarks at the memorial service for the firefighters, Massachusetts Senator Ted Kennedy, no stranger to those waves, spoke about a letter his father had written in 1958 to a friend who had just lost his son. Fourteen years earlier, Ted's oldest brother, Joe, had been killed in World War II. His father referred to that loss when he wrote:

> When one of your loved ones goes out of your life, you think of what he might have done with a few more years, and you wonder what you will do with the rest of yours. Then one day, because there is a world to live in, you find yourself a part of it again, trying to accomplish something—something that he did not have time enough to do. And, perhaps, that is the reason for it all. I hope so.

Grief's pain reminds you that you are alive. It gives you pause to honor the life of the person you loved and to honor the life you have yet to live. To comfort others in their grief, either in the early days or years later, often demands that we be willing to bear silent witness to their pain without needing to make it go away. Grief isn't something that you "get over." It is a feeling you learn to let carry you wherever it is you need to go to feel the love, once more, of the person you miss so much.

Perhaps

❧ *Is this heaven on earth?*

Barbara and Bill had worked in separate cities for the same multi-billion-dollar company—she as a general manager and he as chairman of the board. Their conversations had dealt with business—goals, profits, customer dilemmas, the competition, and caring for employees. However, when they unexpectedly learned that they were each fighting a long-odds battle against cancer, these two colleagues opened the door to a very different level of sharing. One day at lunch, Barbara told Bill how inspired she had been by a recent article she'd read in *Fortune* magazine. In it, General Motors' vice chairman, Harry Pearce, talked about the soul searching he'd gone through during his battle to survive a malignant blood disorder. "We don't have enough high-level executives sharing what's going on with them at a spiritual level when things go wrong," she told Bill. Her comment prompted Bill to open up to her in a new way at one of their annual "check-in" lunches. At our request, he wrote up his thoughts in an essay he titled "Perhaps."

January 6, 2000

It was just a year ago that I had visited with Barbara in my office in St. Louis. She had told me then that the end was in sight, that she had done just about everything she could think of to beat the cancer. We had talked philosophically about lots of things but mostly about life and faith and beliefs and the sometimes unexpected cards that are dealt us during the long and interesting lives we lead. I told her that day that I didn't expect her to die anytime soon and that probably many of our mutual friends might pass from the scene long before she would. I told her that I had thought I might be one of them because I'd had my share of bad stuff—heart problems, prostate cancer, and kidney cancer.

With a bit of bravado I had told her we should plan on having luncheon in New York one year hence. She bravely said, "Sure." Quite surprisingly, the year had rolled around, and here we were at Le Bernardin to have our lunch. The circumstances were still desperate, but she looked great. She told me she was scheduled for exploratory surgery on January 6 and that she felt she had benefited tremendously from a process of meditation that a doctor in San Diego had taught her.

During the course of our conversation, I asked Barbara if she is religious. She said, "No, not really." She said that somehow she still believes in God but doesn't buy into the dogma and the ritual. We found common ground there. I told her that my wife, Jackie, and I had stopped by St. Bartholomew's Church on Park Avenue that morning and said a few prayers for her and others. I told her I found it relatively easy to pray to God even though I don't necessarily believe in all the things we hear from the pulpit. I told her for some time I have thought about the possibility that there is no heaven as many people seem to envision. Maybe we are already in heaven. She listened to my thoughts and made me promise to put them in writing. I told her I would. Today, January 6, 2000, seemed the proper time to do that.

It's not particularly easy for all of us to think of our life on this planet as heaven. Many of us are ill, hungry, infected with AIDS, our homelands emblazoned with strife. Many of us are born into poverty in less desirable parts of the world. Certainly this world of ours is not perfect, or is it? In a wonderful essay written by Samuel Johnson hundreds of years ago, he advanced the theory that the perfect whole is made up of imperfect parts. Perfection is not really perfect.

Is it possible, then, that our world that has so many imperfect parts might, in total, be perfect? Might it, indeed, be heaven? Heaven on earth? How interesting it would be if many of us who envision a life after our current life and our departure from it were wrong. How interesting if the lives we are now leading were lives in heaven. What if we had all lived in another time, in another place, long before now and had, through some process of selection or destiny, been granted another life here on earth in an "earthly heaven."

"But who calls this living?" might a coal miner in western Pennsylvania cry out. "How can this be heaven?" might a starving child in Somalia ask. Or might a very wealthy man, whose unhappiness has caused him to take his life or become dissolute, think of this as heaven? Well, perhaps a second chance in any form, in any place, under any circumstances is, indeed, a gift to be cherished, nurtured, and developed.

Many people who believe in life after death and heaven envision heaven as a place where all of us live in peace and happiness and plenty, where there is no evil, no hunger, no strife, no conflict, no disappointment. A place where every time you drop your line into the water, you promptly catch a fish, where no one need worry about the cold or the heat or the competition from man or beast or virus. Would this really be "heaven"?

Is it possible that our imperfect life is really perfect? Is it possible that we need competition, that we need striving, that we need periodic disappointment, stress, and strain followed by joy and exhilaration? Is defeat sometimes important to us? At the end of the day, when our life is over, is it better to feel exhausted and spent? Is it better to feel we have faced great odds and sometimes overcome them while, at the end, knowing we simply cannot go on forever?

Is, perhaps, our life here on earth—here in earthly heaven—meant to end and end with finality? Should we, perhaps, as we reach the end of "our day" here on earth, close our eyes and smile and thank God for giving us this opportunity of having a second life, a life of heaven on earth? And should we, perhaps, be satisfied—even happy—that a so-called perfect heaven does not await us somewhere else? Perhaps.

Perhaps there is another life for all of us in the memories that others have of us. Perhaps heaven or hell is the memories, good or bad, that people have after we've departed this life. Do they smile when they hear our name? Do they reminisce about the good times we've shared? Do they carry into their own lives and into the lives of others some of the hope we have helped them know? Do we live on in the lives of our family and friends? Do we, perhaps, become a part of them, an even larger, more significant part, after we have physically left than when we were alive and present? Could we have been part of those who have preceded us, and we will now be part of others who will follow us? Perhaps.

I send you my love,

Bill

Each of us carries stories inside of us. Most remain unspoken because we aren't sure how they'd be received. Perhaps we think we can't put them into words. Perhaps we're not sure we're ready to be that vulnerable. I am so grateful that one night Barbara shared Bill's story with me. I'm grateful that he was willing to write it down when he did because a few weeks later, he took a sudden turn for the worse and died. Had he not written it, he would have taken his special view of life with him, unknown to his family, to his friends, and to us.

Bill's story gave me comfort one day when everything was going wrong, or at least not according to my plan. Suddenly I thought of his story and shifted gears to wonder, What if I lived the rest of this day thinking that it was the day from heaven, not the day from hell? Looking through that lens gave me a powerful way of turning what had felt like a hopeless day into one where I felt lucky to be alive here on earth. That is the power of a single story to heal.

Sometimes There Are No Words

There are moments so horrifying that the heart stops, the throat catches, the mind numbs, and there is nothing you can say. That's what happened to most of us on September 11, 2001, when America was attacked by terrorists. Around the world, people saw unimaginable images and experienced feelings beyond any reality we have known. We thought to ourselves, It's not possible that this could happen. It did.

What had meaning for you on that day? Did you gently hold someone's hand? Give someone a shoulder to cry on? Let yourself weep, no matter what? Lend a stranger a cell phone? Give someone a ride or a place to stay? Help someone who was stranded? Visit or call a friend or neighbor who lives alone to offer comfort? Say a prayer? Tell someone, "I love you"? Or were you a silent but caring witness to the fear and grief—yours and that of those around you?

There are moments of loving kindness when the best within us as human beings reaches out to others—across the boundaries of age, race, income, gender, culture, and role. In that moment of our own confusion, fear, anger, or uncertainty, we can choose to wonder, Is there something I can possibly offer another? Can I honestly ask for what I need?

It seems that at times of unspeakable horror, we do have something powerful to offer. We can connect one hurting heart to another with a moment of kindness. A smile to a wary security guard. A thank-you to a firefighter, a police officer, or a volunteer. A "Can I help you?" to a stranger who looks lost. Or we can be a silent, committed witness, paying tribute to those who have died by visiting memorial sites. Paying tribute to the courage of their loved ones who inspire us to pick up the pieces and rebuild our lives. We pause to gather strength in the company of others or to ask for guidance to carry on in the days to come.

There is a powerful gift we can offer or ask for when words fail: undivided attention. Let others pour out their heart—their hurts, questions, hope, bewilderment, or anger. Or as the Reverend Aidan Troy of Belfast, Ireland, told *USA Today* in a story about how other countries have coped with violence, "Find somebody to talk to. I don't mean one of the counselors, but a friend or a group. We are in this together." Or if people aren't able or ready to talk about what has happened—they are stunned into speechlessness—they may find comfort in the stillness of our thoughtful, caring silence.

Being in it together was the choice a group of us made on the morning of the attacks. I was three thousand miles away from home at a West Coast business retreat. In the early hours of uncertainty about what had happened and what it would mean to the world, we wondered whether we could or should continue our meetings. Some of us had flown to the session and were stranded; we all wanted to be home with family. We wondered what was the right thing to do or say.

We took a few moments to close our eyes and send prayers or thoughts to those who needed them. Then we did something rarely done in a business meeting. One person softly asked whether it would be OK if we held hands. People carefully looked around the room to see if that would be uncomfortable for any of the men or women—some of whom had just met. Everyone gently nodded, and we rearranged our chairs so that we could get close enough to silently hold hands around the oblong table. Then the newest member of the firm, the father of a nine-year-old boy, opened his eyes and, choking back tears, said that he didn't know about the rest of us, but he needed a hug. He asked if anyone else wanted one. We slowly stood and awkwardly made our way down to his end of the table, where we quietly held each other. That day, caring for a fellow colleague came from a place beyond words.

After we sat down, the founder said, "I hope that in this company we can always ask for what we need from one another, and if that's to cry, to hug, to vent—that we can be there without being self-conscious." Heads nodded around the table, reassured that the time we had taken to connect in the face of something larger than all of us had somehow made it a little more bearable.

Later that day, we joined with millions of others who felt helpless as we wondered what we could do. In the center of this emotional black hole, New York City's Mayor Giuliani appeared on television and told a watching world to take some time to reach out, especially to the elderly and those living alone. "People are scared," he said, "and they are angry—hold their hand, offer to comfort them."

In the days and weeks and months that follow violence, many of us realize, there is nothing we can do or say to help those who are at ground zero—whether it is the World Trade Center or Oklahoma City or Belfast or Columbine. We ask what we can do to pull together closer to home—at work, in our community, or in our own families. Friends vow to see one another more regularly. Some people realize that they want to donate blood more often, without waiting for a national disaster. Others call spiritual and civic organizations to volunteer. Family members wonder, Maybe we should have a scheduled family night or a telephone reunion once a month. Or as a colleague wrote, "I am wondering how we can sustain a climate of reaching out and connecting with one another without a calamity that somehow gives us permission."

And still others pause to reorder their priorities—perhaps apologizing for a misunderstanding that now no longer seems important. For some, an unexpected disaster makes us want to clear the air of anything that violates our spirit or the spirit of others.

After a tragedy, especially a violent one, we see with different eyes, hear with different ears, and lend a gentler touch as we discover the strength in our vulnerability. As one veteran Wall Street leader responded to a newscaster's question the day the New York Stock Exchange reopened, "No, we didn't used to be a 'huggy' place. But now," he said, as cameras showed colleagues tearfully hugging one another as they discover who is still alive, "now we are."

Our commitment to bear witness to the suffering enables us to unite, to create a bridge across the river of our fears. We set about rebuilding a hurting heart, a cratered city, a shattered school, a crumbling company, or a devastated nation with the tender hope that we may heal—one breath, one hour, one brick, one hug, or one whispered blessing at a time.

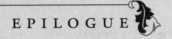

In the End

Healing Takes Time

WHETHER IT INVOLVES THE LOSS OF A JOB, HEALTH, OR A LOVED ONE, please remember: healing takes time. We want to rush it. To get back to being normal. To forget. To be happy again. But we can't go back. Can't undo. Can't make it fit our schedule. And as much as they'd like to, neither can our friends and family who are trying to help us through this tough time.

The pain of loss is a many-layered thing.

Healing is about gaining access to the places in your heart that you have shut down. It's about being alone. Being a hermit. Being with others. It's about therapy, journals, walks on the beach, talks with friends, self-help books, and books to help you forget.

"Healing is a twenty-four-hour-a-day process," my friend Jeannie said when I asked her to talk to me about how you know you are finally healing.

To me, healing is like a garden: the seeds you plant are growing underneath. You can't see anything for a while until after enough rain, sun, time, feeding, and weeding—then something new begins to grow.

Healing takes courage—to move forward with life when sometimes the pain seems more than we can bear. We need friends who can listen to us be numb, be in denial, have second thoughts, be angry, be hyperbusy, ignore them, need them, cry or be stoic, and maybe even help us laugh at it all. We may cycle back and forth, even fooling ourselves into thinking that we are past being upset over a song, a thought, a memory, words—and then wham! We feel as if we have rolled right back down to the bottom of the mountain we thought we had just climbed. We need to feel safe enough to be messy and irrational with you one day and know that you'll still be our friend the day after.

Often we try to help someone through a difficult time by saying things like "Time heals all wounds" or "You'll look back and be grateful for what you learned" or "You'll survive" or "It could have been worse" or "What doesn't kill you makes you stronger." Well, all of these sayings may be true, but when someone is in the healing process, whether it's fast or slow, it's very personal. No two people are alike—whether widowed, divorced, fired, diagnosed with an illness, relocating, or dealing with a difficult situation at work. We all have our own stories—histories—that come into play when we're in pain. We can't always know what's causing others to hurt or what will help them heal. That's why they need us to be patient. Oh, so patient!

Sometimes we get the comfort we need from our friends and family. Sometimes, oddly enough, they let us down. We can be surprised at the kindness of a stranger, the wisdom of a good listener—you know, that stranger we meet on a plane. Whether intentional or random, kindness can touch us in ways we didn't expect possible. It comes as an unexpected gift.

Healing conversations? Sooner or later we have one with ourselves. We ask, Why did it happen? We think, If only . . . We replay what did or didn't happen. We wonder what higher purpose was there in all of this. We ask, What have I learned? Where do I go from here?

We may even ask a Higher Power, the Universe, Spirit, or God—whoever we believe that power to be—to talk to us, to guide us. Or we may turn away. We may not be able to hear, or we may feel that there is no one listening. We may or may not like or believe what we hear from friends or from a higher guide. It may take us time to understand how to follow the guidance that comes. It can also take years to understand what role we may have unconsciously played in contributing to a once painful situation—for example, when we didn't speak up when someone hurt us or when we didn't leave an unhealthy work environment. We need friends who won't wonder why it took us so long to see what we couldn't see.

And finally, healing conversations are about forgiveness. We may be able to forgive others before they die or before we die. Or we may not be ready to forgive or may not take that chance in time. We may find a way to forgive them or to ask for their forgiveness long after they are gone. Sometimes we don't really heal until we forgive ourselves.

Whether you are a friend, a colleague, a family member, or stranger we meet by chance, being with us as we heal takes patience, a sense of humor, and the grace and courage to give us perspective. To tell us what we may not want to hear. To *pause* long enough before speaking to find a way to help us hear what we fear the most.

And when the healing begins to take hold—whether it is the light you see in our eyes once again, the energy you hear restored in our voice, the enthusiasm you sense we have for our work, or the step in a new direction we can't even see we took—your reflecting back to us what we may not always be able to see, hear, or sense can be a godsend!

Reflecting back what he'd heard was the gift one friend gave another months into her recovery from a difficult time. Unexpectedly getting her answering machine when he called, he'd heard something in her voice and wanted to make sure she was aware of what it signaled to him. "I can hear that you are no longer being ripped and torn. The healing is beginning." Until that moment, overwhelmed by shock and pain, his friend had not realized that the healing had begun. There are times when healing is nothing more, and nothing less, than offering the gentle gift of awareness.

APPRECIATIONS

Maybe you've seen yourself or someone you care about in these stories from friends, strangers, family and from me. One thing is certain, this book would not have gotten into your hands without the chain of connections that was created when one person showed up to either help me through a rough time or to introduce me to someone else with an inspiring story. What follows is not only an appreciation to the people who helped create these caring connections, but also an appreciation for the Force that put each of us in the other's life at *just the right time*.

When my job took me on the road after my mom's death, I coped with the grieving by telling stories—about awkward or unexpected moments such as what happened when we scattered her ashes. People asked me to write the stories down because they wanted to pass them along to comfort others going through difficult times. Thank you to my brothers, James and Ken, and my sister, Laurie, for graciously letting me tell our stories.

Nine years after Mom died, I was divorced, living alone and learning to cope with winters by the sea. I often turned to a neighbor and her family for practical survival skills that somehow, to their amusement, I'd never learned. One day she heard me say, once too often, that *some day* I was going to write a book to help people help others. "I'll give you eight months to get it started. If you don't get started by then, you never will!" Thank you to my adopted "godmother" for her loving candor, and to her family who put up with the hundreds of hours she spent reviewing stories—helping me understand what was important and what wasn't.

I never would have met my neighbor if it hadn't been for Liz Kay. On a "raining cats and dogs" October day, Liz drove me around from town to town to help me find a place by the sea to live. Thank you, Liz, for sticking by me— *for years.*

Someone else who sticks by me when there is often no light in the tunnel is my colleague and coach for life, Logan Loomis. Yes, Logan of the *Sugarplum* story who patiently helps me see the light.

Among the most powerful healing conversations I've ever had took place with Bill Armstrong—massage therapist, teacher, and friend. Bill, my thanks to you go beyond thanks . . . Then there are the other healers in my life who tended to me during uncertain times: Dr. Bob Videyko, Dr. Joyce Adamson, Dr. Anthony DiSciullo, John Wile (and the caring nurses and staff who work for them), and James Waslaski. Dr. Rudi Ansbacher and Will Calmas were early believers in the book's mission to nurture our capacity to listen to and care for one another. Thanks also go to my compassionate "computer doctor," Andy Agapow and the ever-patient Keith Harris at Choice Graphics.

Other friends, who are an adopted extended family, have helped me turn the corner at times when I felt a bit lost: Moshe Hammer, Fred Norwood,

Emilia Nuccio, Santina Scialfa, Jeannie Lindheim, Pat and Jim, Alice and Byrd, Wyllys and Marianne, Rick and Annie, Shelley and Ed Hobson, JoAnn and Ken Lickel, Vail, Peter Shaplen, Leslie Berger, David Anderson, Sandee Adams, Neal Shiffman, Reverend Aram Marashlian and Bobby—thank you. I also have an abiding appreciation for Christopher who will always be my friend and for Rasmani Deborah Orth whose teachings last a lifetime.

Without the storytellers there would be no book! They had the courage to let me listen in to what they said, what they meant and what they didn't yet know how to say. Thank you all—*you know who you are*. A special thanks to Barbara Riefle who often put her life on the line with me to share her will to live and to help others in the process.

What does it take for one person to be willing to help another? Fortunately I was given opportunities to learn this by my bosses and colleagues at CBS WEEI, Newsradio, by the late Senator Paul Tsongas and his staff, and by WBZ-TV and Westinghouse Broadcasting. Thank you especially to Mike Wheeler of WEEI, former WBZ-TV General Manager, Sy Yanoff, and to GroupW TV's President Emeritus, Tom Goodgame, who supported me in taking chances on behalf of those whose voices needed to be heard. Blessings also go to the dedicated news editors, producers, on-air talent, and staff who made the Designated Driver Program and the For Kids' Sake campaign realities—especially Amy McGregor-Radin, Kim Harbin, Andrew Radin, Lois Roach, Amy Freidland, Scott Samenfeld, and Randy Covington.

This book wouldn't have found its publisher had it not been for the personal growth programs at Kripalu Center for Yoga and Health, where I learned what it takes to set aside our judgments, try to listen from the heart, and found my way to a true kindred spirit, Jan Nickerson. Years later this steadfast friend introduced me to Karen Speerstra, a former publisher, who referred me to Doris Michaels, who became my agent, who referred me to Gerry Sindell, who introduced the book to Sheryl Fullerton, who became my thoughtful editor and spirit guide at Jossey-Bass. A special appreciation for the efforts of Jessica Egbert, Jesica Church, Mark Kerr, Joanne Clapp Fullagar, Denise Carrigg, and the many other Jossey-Bass team members who devoted special effort to helping this book reach readers. Sue Little and Paul Abruzzi of Jabberwocky Bookstore have been steadfast supporters, encouraging me to hang in there during the search for the right publisher.

John Scherer and his wife Catharine became unforgettable clients, mentors, and friends who introduced me to Jan Smith, the dedicated and courageous founder of the Center for Authentic Leadership. Many stories in this book come from conversations that participants open-heartedly shared with me.

Another important source of stories is my clients. Thank you for putting your newfound communication skills to work even when it's challenging. Carol Cone and Jens Bang were pioneers when they introduced their teams to the idea of having courageous conversations. A special thanks to the Saunders family, not only for putting the principles of healing conversations to work at home and at the office, but also for giving me the perfect place to write when I needed it most.

As you can imagine, it takes thousands of hours to compose a book. Much of that time was spent at the computer writing—with the healing sounds of Peter Kater's music in the background. Thank you, Peter, for recording *Essence* and *Compassion*.

And finally, thank you to the many strangers whose intentional kindness meant more to me than you will ever know. One of those strangers was Joe

Stanganelli, a Staples print shop manager who invested extra care in printing the first draft of the manuscript so that it would capture the heart of a publisher. I wasn't just another copy order that day; he sensed what this book could mean. Who knows what a caring act can mean to someone who is having *one of those days?*

RESOURCES

Sometimes the best gift you can give is the gift of understanding. One way to do that is to read a book, listen to a tape, or attend a program about the challenge faced by you or someone you're trying to comfort. It's one way to learn more about what you or the other person needs. All of the resources listed are also suitable as gifts—perhaps helping you or someone you know feel heartened and less alone. The selections are a sampling of what my friends and I have found to be especially helpful. You will find many more by searching Web sites, libraries, bookstores, and your friends' bookshelves.

BOOKS

Everyday Sacred: A Woman's Journey Home by Sue Bender (HarperCollins, 1996). An uplifting book that helps us find meaning and renewal in life's smallest moments.

How to Heal Depression by Harold Bloomfield and Peter McWilliams (Prelude Press, 1994). A practical primer written in everyday language.

The Healing Runes: Tools for the Recovery of Body, Mind, Heart, and Soul by Ralph Blum and Susan Loughan (St. Martin's Press, 1995). This book, with its bag of rune pieces, makes healing an interactive joy. Based on Celtic traditions, the book helps readers fine-tune their capacity for intuitive self-healing.

First You Have to Row a Little Boat by Richard Bode (Warner Books, 1993). The author's eloquent story of how to navigate life when you're feeling lost.

Simple Abundance: A Daybook of Comfort and Joy by Sara Ban Breathnach (Warner Books, 1995). A wonderful book to help anyone find a daily anchor in an upside-down world.

Transitions: Making Sense of Life's Changes by William Bridges (Addison-Wesley, 1980). A must read for anyone going through or supporting another during a loss of a job, relationship, or way of life.

Don't Sweat the Small Stuff . . . and It's All Small Stuff by Richard Carlson (Hyperion, 1997). Offers simple but powerful ways to cope with the multitude of stresses in our lives.

The Places That Scare You: A Guide to Fearlessness in Difficult Times by Pema Chödrön (Shambhala, 2001). Helps readers move through difficult circumstances with an outlook of loving-kindness toward oneself and others.

How to Survive the Loss of a Love by Melba Colgrove, Harold Bloomfield, and Peter McWilliams (Prelude Press, 1976). Helps keep one's spirit alive during the often overwhelming stages of loss and healing after a relationship ends—whether through death, divorce, or breaking up.

The Enigma of Suicide by George Howe Colt (Summit Books, 1991). An investigation into the causes of suicide and the approaches to prevention and healing.

The Power of Apology: A Healing Strategy to Transform All Your Relationships by Beverly Engel (Wiley, 2001). Teaches how to become a more humble, compassionate, and empathetic human being.

Forgiveness Is a Choice: A Step-by-Step Process for Resolving Anger and Restoring Hope by Robert Enright (American Psychological Association Life Tools, 2001). Helps us appreciate the roadblocks to forgiveness and slowly learn how to overcome them.

The Verbally Abusive Relationship: How to Recognize It and How to Respond by Patricia Evans (Adams Media, 1992). A lifesaving book that teaches how to recognize the subtle and not so subtle signs of verbal abuse and what to do about it. See also www.verbalabuse.com.

Verbal Abuse Survivors Speak Out: On Relationship and Recovery by Patricia Evans (Adams Media, 1993). A powerful book to help someone pick up the pieces of life after ending a verbally abusive relationship. Outlines explicit healing practices and helps a reader understand what someone has gone through. A must read for friends, family, and survivors.

The Language of Goodbye by Maribeth Fischer (Dutton, 2001). A lovely novel that puts into words what the heart can't say about letting go of the past while seeking a future inevitably shaped by what we have endured.

Rebuilding: When Your Relationship Ends by Bruce Fisher (Impact, 1981). A handbook for the divorcing and divorced (and their friends and family) that helps us understand the pitfalls and possibilities in starting over.

Backing Down the Ladder by Andy Fleming (New Visions Press,1998). A collection of poems filled with irony, humor, and compassion. The reader joins Andy in exploring the past and the future at the cusp of midlife.

It Was on Fire When I Lay Down on It by Robert Fulgham (Ivy, 1988). I recommend *all* of Robert Fulgham's books as wonderful opportunities for respite when you or someone you know faces troubling times.

Suicide: Prevention, Intervention, Postvention by Rabbi Earl Grollman (Beacon Press, 1988). Gives advice on recognizing warning signs, intervening, and comforting those who have lost a loved one to suicide.

Prepare for Surgery: Heal Faster by Peggy Huddleston (Angel River Press, 1996). Patients and their friends, medical team, and family get practical advice on how to prepare for and heal from surgery—physically, emotionally, and spiritually. A great gift. See also www. healfaster.com.

If the Buddha Dated: A Handbook for Finding Love on a Spiritual Path by Charlotte Kasl (Compass/Penguin, 1999). Helps readers who are trying to find the courage to start over again in their search for a loving companion.

A Path with Heart: A Guide Through the Perils and Promises of Spiritual Life by Jack Kornfield (Bantam, 1993). A valuable and thorough guide for increasing your capacity for compassion—for yourself and others.

On Death and Dying: What the Dying Have to Teach Doctors, Nurses, Clergy, and Their Own Families by Elisabeth Kübler-Ross (Touchstone, 1969). A book to read and reread to remind us of the stages of dying. It helps us have greater appreciation for the needs of the dying and the living.

Healing into Life and Death by Stephen Levine (Anchor/Doubleday, 1987). This book offers ways to be with pain and grief through merciful awareness of our own discomfort, compassion, meditation, and forgiveness. Extremely helpful for patients, friends, and family where illness or a chronic condition is present.

A Year to Live: How to Live This Year As If It Were Your Last by Stephen Levine (Bell Tower/Harmony, 1997). A guide for anyone who wants to learn how to appreciate living life to its fullest no matter what difficulties land on your plate.

Way of the Peaceful Warrior: A Book That Changes Lives by Dan Millman (Kramer, 1980). This classic is based on the story of a world-champion athlete whose injury challenges him to find a new path to living a full life.

The Essene Book of Days, 2001 by Danaam and Danaan Parry (Earthstewards Network, 2000). A collection of meditations, including the unforgettable essay "Fear of Transformation," which articulates the reasons why we find it hard to let go of what we have in order to step out into the unknown.

Kitchen Table Wisdom: Stories That Heal by Naomi Remen (Riverhead Books, 1996). Dr. Remen shares painful and poignant stories—hers and her patients'—to help patients, doctors, and the rest of us appreciate what it means to be human.

The Four Agreements by Don Miguel Ruiz (Amber Allen, 1997). Teaches us how to consciously manage our reactions—to ourselves and to others—so that we're better able to ask for what we need and to offer what is called for in healthy relationships.

The Courage to Grieve: Creative Living, Recovery, and Growth Through Grief by Judy Tatelbaum (HarperCollins, 1984). The author helps us understand how to grow from having the courage to mourn the losses that we inevitably experience. A compassionate, optimistic aid for those who are grieving and those supporting them.

Crazy Time: Surviving Divorce and Building a New Life by Abigail Trafford (HarperCollins, 1982). This book answers the question many ask while going through a divorce: Am I ever going to get through this? True stories take you through the stages of the breakup and help you avoid getting stuck for too long in any one of them.

Illuminata: Thoughts, Prayers, and Rites of Passage by Marianne Williamson (Random House, 1994). A gift to give and receive that provides ways to bring prayer into everyday life—to heal the body, relationships, and the spirit.

Remembering Well: Rituals for Celebrating Life and Mourning Death by Sarah York (Jossey-Bass, 2000). A comprehensive collection of stories and practical suggestions for creating ceremonies to commemorate a loved one's life, especially in situations where we feel awkward or unprepared.

Wherever You Go, There You Are: Mindfulness Meditations in Everyday Life by Jon Kabat-Zinn (Hyperion, 1994). Discover how to quiet your mind when pressures pull you in all directions. Especially valuable for learning how to be with distress, discomfort, confusion, pain, and silence.

TAPES

Why People Don't Heal . . . and How They Can by Carolyn Myss, based on the best-selling book of the same name (Harmony Books, 1997). I highly recommend this book on tape in which the author's self-deprecating humor and bluntness help us understand why we keep holding on to the pain of what happened in our past and what it will take for us to heal.

ART

Richard Bohn, creator of healing hearts pottery sculpture and author of "Burnt Offerings" (featured in this book). P.O. Box 11821, Spokane, WA 99211.

MUSIC

This is a sampling of music that you or others may find comforting during difficult times.

The Yearning by Michael Hoppe and Tim Wheater (WEA/Atlantic, 1996). Ethereal and elegant alto flute music draws you in to a reverie.

Michael's Music: A Michael Jones Retrospective (Narada Productions, 1990). Uplifting piano music.

Compassion and *Essence* recorded by Peter Kater, composer and musician. Both CDs create an especially soothing effect. (Source Music, P.O. Box 1109, Warrenton, VA 20188. www.peterkater.com.)

For God Alone by Mark Kelso (Kelso Productions, 1988). Harmonies for meditation, yoga, or quiet hope.

When You Wish upon a Star by Daniel Kobialka (Li-Sem Enterprises, 1988). A collection of lullabies.

Return to the Heart by David Lanz (Narada Productions, 1991). Powerful piano tour of the journey of a heart.

In the Falling Dark by Dave Mallet (Vanguard, 1995). Poignant and optimistic folk music with lyrics that give hope for light at the end of the tunnel.

Days Like This by Van Morrison (Exile Productions, 1995). You can't help but sing along to these tunes when you are feeling blue and want a little company.

Healing Hands of Time by Willie Nelson (EMI Records, 1994). The title song, "Healing Hands of Time," offers comfort when you're wondering when the pain will fade.

A soothing selection from classical artists including Beethoven, Mozart, Pachelbel, and Albinoni can be found on a 1988 Philips I Musici recording, no. 410 606 2.

CENTERS FOR CONTINUING EDUCATION

Participating in programs is one way to deepen our understanding of ourselves, family, friends, and colleagues. These centers offer opportunities to advance communication skills and to move past painful roadblocks. You can go with someone who is having a difficult time, attend by yourself, or as some people do, give such an experience as a gift to someone seeking the chance to grow in the company of others.

Center for Authentic Leadership. An international community of leaders in development. Provides multiyear programs that develop a deep capacity to listen (to yourself and to others) and to heal the past so that you can create a future based on your unique gifts. In Atlanta. (800) 864-0431. www.authenticleadership.com.

Center for Work and the Human Spirit. An ongoing series of powerful yet practical personal and professional development programs seeking to bring intentional communication into the workplace at all levels. (800) 727-9115. www.sygroupinc.com.

Kripalu Center for Yoga and Health. A spiritually based retreat and renewal center in Lenox, Massachusetts, where you can learn many paths for listening—to the body, the mind, and the heart. Practical group-based yoga, meditation, and personal growth programs vary from season to season. (800) 741-7353.

Omega Institute for Holistic Studies. A nonprofit learning center in Rhinebeck, New York, offering programs to help participants explore a variety of approaches to better physical and spiritual health. (800) 944-1001. www.eomega.org.

Wave Work Institute. Offers training and certification for professionals in the helping and healing fields. The focus is on new ways to help people transform and develop their access to inner healing. (877) WAVEWORK (928-3967). www.wavework.com.

OUTREACH

Centering Corporation. A nonprofit bereavement resource center providing access to books, tapes, booklets, and workshops on grieving—whether you are a child, parent, caregiver, or healing professional dealing with death, illness, infertility, or disability. (402) 553-1200. www.centering.org.

Compassionate Friends. A national nonprofit organization offering support and guidance to families (and those supporting them) who have lost a child of any age. (877) 969-0010. www.compassionatefriends.org.

Faith in Action. A national interfaith, volunteer, caregiving program of The Robert Wood Johnson Foundation. Grants fund community volunteer programs that help people who are chronically ill, frail, elderly, or disabled maintain a level of independence in their daily lives. To volunteer, receive care, or start a Faith in Action program, (877) FAITH11 or www.FIAVolunteers.org.

National Hospice Foundation. Can help you find answers to questions such as how to find hospice care, what to expect, and medical coverage for such care. National Hospice Foundation, 1700 Diagonal Rd., Suite 300, Alexandria, VA 22314. (703) 516-4928; e-mail: nhf@nhpco.org; www.nhpco.org.

THE AUTHOR

Nance Guilmartin is an award-winning broadcast journalist known for discerning the essence and heart of any story. As a former Westinghouse Broadcasting senior executive, she helped launch national community awareness initiatives, including the Designated Driver Program and the For Kids' Sake and Time to Care campaigns. She served as press secretary to U.S. Senator Paul Tsongas of Massachusetts and helped him win his Senate seat. Today Nance is a business consultant helping leaders unlock innovation and impossible possibilities by learning what to say and how to listen, strengthening what is often their weakest link: communication.

Frequently asked to speak, lead workshops, and facilitate retreats, Nance leverages organizational change with her insights into the art of listening and the power of timely, courageous conversations. You may contact her at P.O. Box 796, Rowley, MA 01969, or at www.nanceguilmartin.com.

INDEX

C

setting, 80–83; importance of, 5, 13–15, 76; power of in workplace, 127–130, 137–140; without judgment, 7, 113, 269–270
Living alone, 193–195
Loss, unexpected, 236–239
Loughan, S., 304
Lymphoma, 212

M
Mallet, D., 310
Managed care, and time for patients, 81–83
Massachusetts Restaurant Association, 273
McWilliams, P., 77, 304
Medical test results, 58–62
Meditation, 30–31, 116, 118
Mementos, disposal of, 258–259
Memories, 35–38, 52
Mergers, 145–146
Messages, of comfort, 20–21
Michael's Music: A Michael Jones Retrospective (recording), 310
Millman, D., 64, 307
Miscarriage, 13–15
Morrison, V., 310
Moving, 35–39
Music, suggestions for, 310–311
Myss, C., 87, 309

N
Nancamp, 274
Nathan, N., 163–164
National Hospice Foundation, 313
Near-death experiences, 100–104
Nelson, W., 311
Newcomers, how to help, 38–39

O
Obituary, writing of before death, 242–244
Oklahoma City bombing, 288
Omega Institute for Holistic Studies, 312
On Death and Dying: What the Dying Have to Teach Doctors, Nurses, Clergy, and Their Own Families (Kübler-Ross), 307
One Year to Live (Levine), 228
Outreach organizations, 312–313

P
Pain: comforting others in, 88, 115–119; and importance of listening, 13–15; living with, 84–88; patience and, 76–78
Parry, D., 148, 307
A Path with Heart: A Guide Through the Perils and Promises of Spiritual Life (Kornfield), 307
Patience, and enduring pain, 76–78